221 FACTS ABOUT EARTH

MANOJ PUBLICATIONS

221 Facts About Earth

Publishers:

MANOJ PUBLICATIONS

761, Main Road, Burari, Delhi-110084

Mobile : 09999476076, 9868112194,
          8178823569, 8178854810

Email   : info@manojpublications.com

For online shopping visit our website :
www.sawanonlinebookstore.com

ISBN : 978-81-310-2460-7

CONTENTS

1. Evolution of the Earth

Evolution is a process of gradual growth and development of life on the Earth from simple to complex form. Evolution of the Earth started around 4.5 billion years ago, when our solar system took shape due to the massive explosion of a small molecular ball called the Big Bang. During the evolution phase, the Earth went through many changes, for example: invasion of the land by oceans, uplift of mountains, erosion and ice age. Some of the initial forms of life were unable to withstand these extreme conditions and got extinct. But fortunately, they left some tiny traces of their existence behind in the form of fossils. These traces helped geologists to put together a general idea of the timeline of life.

Evolution of Earth

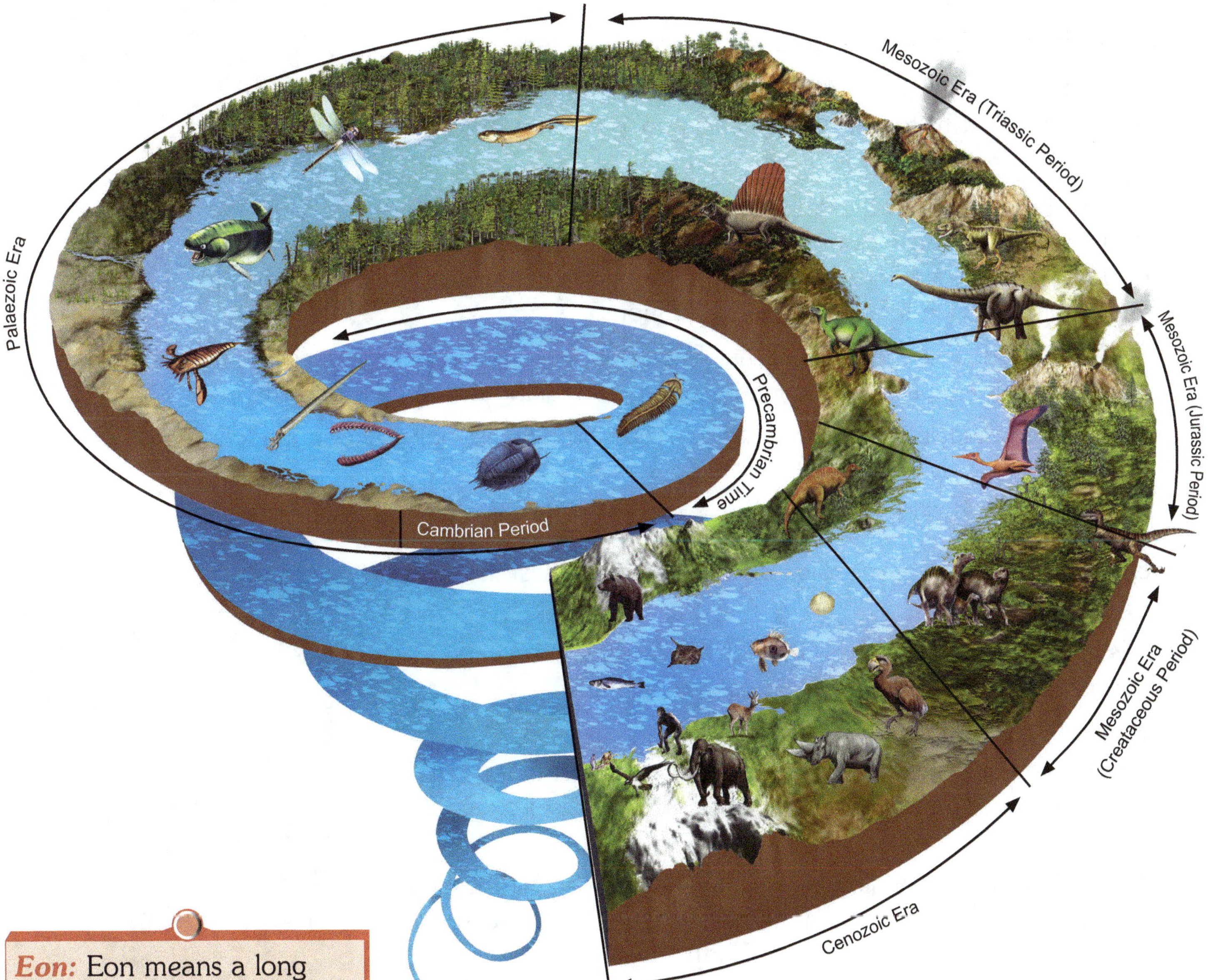

Eon: Eon means a long period of time which is indefinite or whose duration is not exactly known.

2. Precambrian Time

The period from which the formation of the Earth started is known as the Precambrian time. The term Precambrian is an informal term and is used for both time and rocks.

Time Period: This period extends from about 4.5 billion years ago to the beginning of the Cambrian period.

Features:

- A big part of history is covered in this period, starting from the creation of the planet to the appearance of multi-celled life forms.
- Precambrian period is divided into three eons: the Hadean, the Archean, and the Proterozoic.
- The oldest known glaciation occurred during the Precambrian time.

3. Hadean Eon

Hadean Eon is the first division of the Precambrian time.

Time Period: The duration of this eon is between 4.5 billion (beginning of the Earth) to 4.0 billion years ago.

Features:

- This is the time when the solar system, including the Earth had just formed from the cloud of dust and gases. Those clouds and gaseous material started converting into liquid. The condition of the Earth was so bad that the time period was named as Hadean after 'hades'. Hades is a Greek word, which refers to hellish conditions.
- In this period, the Earth's external heat was the result of meteorites hitting the Earth with tremendous force. This heat contributed to the melting of the young Earth.
- The development of the Earth's atmosphere and oceans took place in Hadean eon.

4. Archean Eon

Archean eon or Archaeozoic is the second division of the Precambrian time.

Time Period: It began around 4 billion years ago and extended till the beginning of Proterozoic eon 2.5 billion years ago.

Features:

- There were many volcanic gases in the atmosphere, but the dominating gas was carbon dioxide and the level of oxygen was very low.
- The first photosynthesising organisms had evolved by the end of this eon. They started to produce oxygen, which eventually changed the environment on the Earth.
- In the Archean eon, the rocks were mostly igneous or metamorphic, but from this period onwards the sedimentary rocks also started forming in the ocean.

5. Proterozoic Eon

Stromatolites

Proterozoic eon is the third and last eon of the Precambrian time.

Time Period: This eon extends from 2.5 billion to 600 million years ago.

Features:

- During this eon, the Earth started getting its present day shape and landforms arose. The Earth experienced global glaciation for the first time.
- Life began to appear from simple single-cell organisms to more advanced single-cell organisms, which led to a diversification in the types of organisms found in the ocean. This increased the amount of oxygen in the atmosphere.
- The oldest fossils include: algae, jellyfish and worms.
- Stromatolite is one of the oldest forms of blue green algae, present today. They are found in abundance in Sharks Bay in western Australia.

6. Palaeozoic Era

The Precambrian time was followed by the Palaeozoic era. The first major period of this era was Cambrian Period (600 million to 500 million years). Major fossils show their earliest occurrence from this period.

Time Period: It extends from around 600 million to 225 million years ago.

Features:

- The Palaeozoic is best known for explosion of life on the Earth. This era witnessed fossils ranging from many primitive life forms up to some of the earliest land-dwelling animals. Fish, amphibians and early reptiles appeared during this era.
- Continents were assembled as a supercontinent called Pannotia at the beginning of the Palaeozoic area.
- This was at the end of the global ice age (glaciatio

7. Mesozoic Era

The Palaeozoic era was followed by the Mesozoic e was 'the era of reptiles', when dinosaurs ruled the world

It was the time of geologic and biological transition divided into three major periods: Triassic, Jurassic Cretaceous.

Time Period: This era started 225 million years ago lasted up to 70 million years ago.

Features:

- During this era the continents began to move into day configurations.
- A distinct modernisation of life-forms occurred, partly because of the demise of several Palaeozoic

organisms. This extinction wiped out about 95% of all marine life and 70% of terrestrial animals. The era ended with 'the great extinction' which marked the end of the dinosaurs as the Cenozoic era began.

Triassic: This period started 225 million years ago, and lasted for 45 million years. Evolution of many land reptiles, including the dinosaurs took place in this period.

Jurassic: This period started 180 million years ago and lasted for 45 million years. Several large dinosaurs evolved in this period. The oldest bird fossils are from the Jurassic period.

Cretaceous: This period started 135 million years ago and lasted for 65 million years. By the end of this period, the dinosaurs became extinct. Modern plants such as magnolia, fig and poplar evolved during this period.

8. Cenozoic Era

Cenozoic era is the third major era after Precambrian period. The name Cenozoic was derived from the Greek word meaning 'recent life'. This era is also called the 'age of mammals'.

Time Period: This era started around 70 million years ago, extending to the present time, in which we live.

Features:
♦ Flowering plants and insects became widespread in this era and a relationship between insects and flowers also developed.
♦ The separation of continents that had begun at the end of the Mesozoic era continued.

Charles Darwin

9. Planet Earth

The Earth is a big ball-shaped moving body, mostly made up of rocks. It is the only planet in the solar system which has life. Life on the Earth became possible because of the availability of oxygen, the moderate temperature, the availability of water and the favourable atmosphere. It is the fifth largest planet of the solar system and is the third planet from the Sun. When the Earth is viewed from space, it looks like a mixture of blue, white, green and brown colours. The reason behind this is the presence of water, land and plants. The Earth is surrounded by a layer of gases.

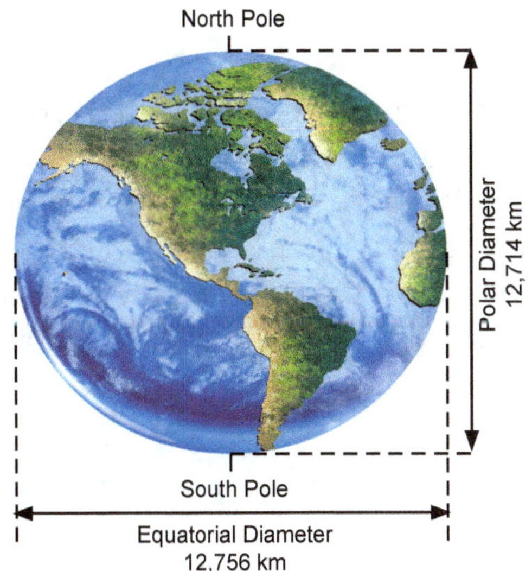

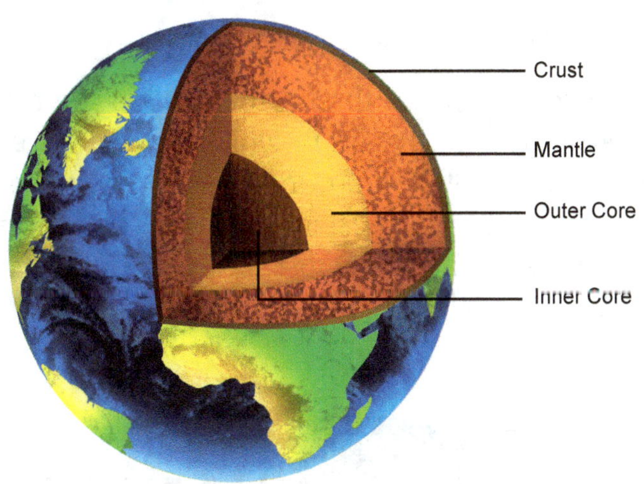

10. Shape of the Earth

The Earth is oblate spheroid (bulging at equators and flattening at poles) in shape. However, in the early days it was thought to be a flat piece of land. A major discovery with respect to the circumference and shape of the Earth was done in 25 BC. A Greek mathematician, named Eratosthenes, calculated the circumference of the Earth using the idea of a round shape. The diameter of the Earth is about 12,714 km, and the Earth bulges at the equator. Sir Isaac Newton carried out the analysis related to the bulges of the Earth at the equator, for the first time.

11. Structure of the Earth

When studied closely, we find that the Earth has a layered structure. It is made up of three main layers: the crust, the mantle and the core. The crust is the outermost part, the mantle is the middle layer and the core is the centremost layer. As we travel towards the core of the Earth, the temperature increases. On an average, the temperature increases about $1°F$ ($1°F = -17.2°C$) for every 60 feet distance downwards. The rocks present beneath the surface of the Earth are very hot due to high pressure.

12. The Crust

The crust is the outermost part of the Earth and is also called the lithosphere. The crust of the Earth is divided into two parts: continental crust and oceanic crust. The land part or continents are formed by the continental crust. The continental crust is made up of rocks that consist of primarily silica (Si) and aluminia (Al) and hence called 'sial'. On an average, the thickness of this part of the crust varies from 35 to 70 km. The second part is the ocean crust, which is situated below the oceans. The

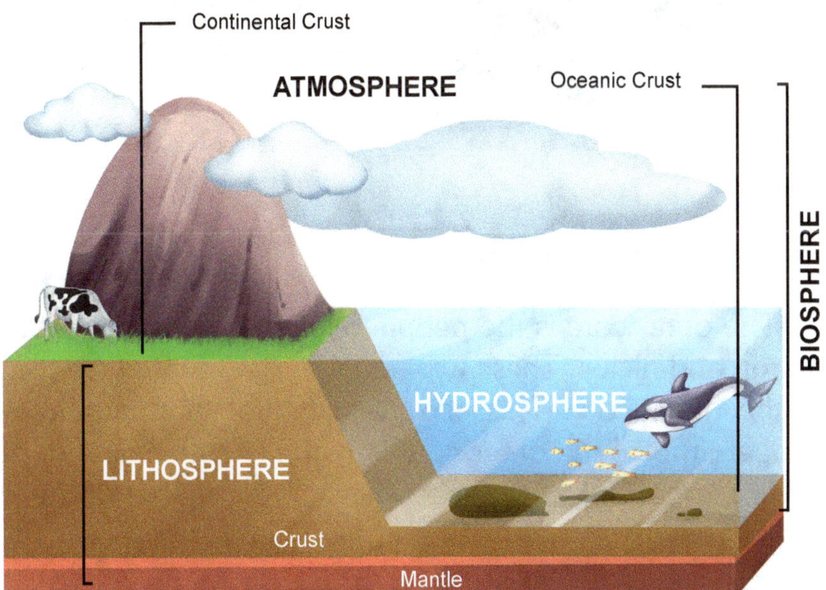

oceanic crust consists of silica (Si) and magnesium (Mg) and hence called 'sima'. The ocean crust is thin (5-10 km) and dense in comparison to continental crust.

Lithosphere: Lithosphere is composed of the outer layer of the Earth's crust and the upper mantle. It is made up of rock slabs called crustal plates (tectonic plates).

Hydrosphere: The parts of the crust that hold water is called hydrosphere. It is comprised of oceans, seas, rivers, lakes and streams.

13. The Mantle

The second layer of the Earth is called the mantle. It lies between the crust and the core. This is the thickest layer of the Earth which constitutes up to 83% of the Earth's volume. It extends up to a depth of 2900 to 3000 km from the crust to the core. This layer is composed of a dark, dense, igneous (silicate) rock with magnesium and iron, and a gooey layer. A gooey layer is a hot layer of magma. The upper mantle and the crust surface is mainly composed of broken pieces called the tectonic plates. These tectonic plates interact with one another and give rise to earthquakes, volcanic eruptions, etc. on the Earth.

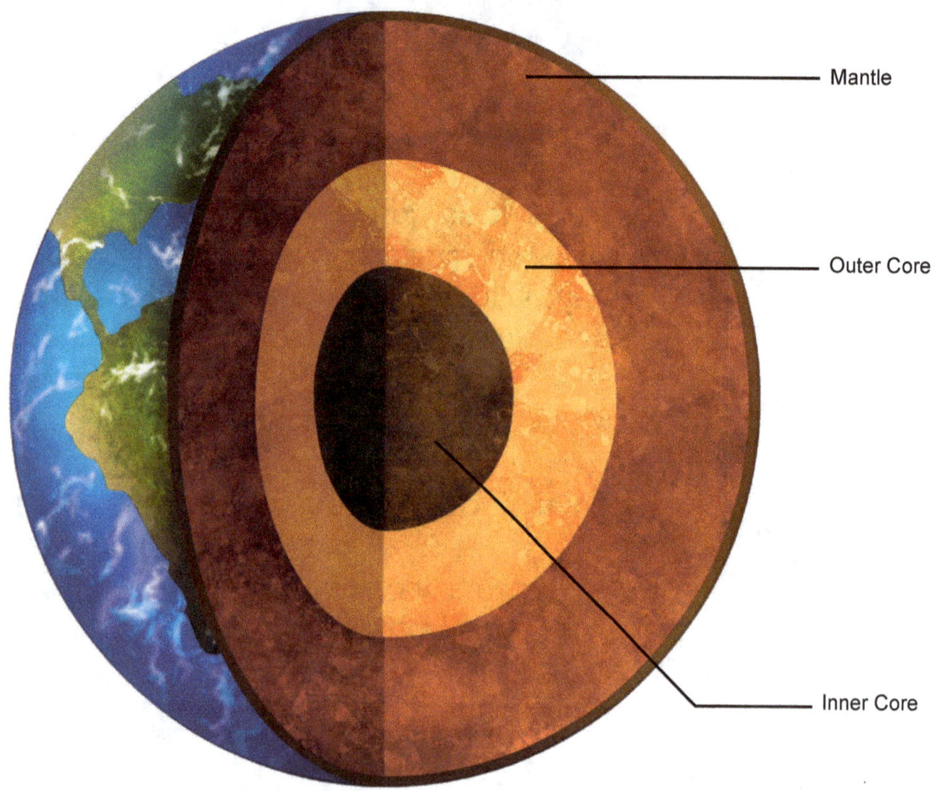

14. The Core

The core is the innermost, deepest, and the hottest layer of the Earth. It is believed that this part of the Earth is made up of two layers: an inner core (dark brown) and an outer core (yellow). The inner core is solid and the outer core is super-heated liquid molten lava. This part is the hottest and the densest layer of the Earth due to the presence of the lava. The core is a thin layer that constitutes up to 16% of the planet's volume. It is mainly composed of iron and nickel.

15. Outer Core

The outer core is the peripheral part of the core. This part of the Earth's core is mostly composed of iron and nickel. These two metals are present in the form of an alloy (a mixture of metallic elements) in the outer core. This alloy is very hot (temperature between 4000°-5000°C), due to which the temperature of the outer core is high. The thickness of outer core is about 2300 km. The outer core is very important as the movement of the metals of this core creates a magnetic field on the Earth.

16. Inner Core

The inner core is the deepest layer of the Earth. The same as outer core, the inner core is made up of nickel and iron, with the ratio of iron on the higher side. The thickness of the inner core is about 1200 km. The iron present in the core is extremely hot (temperature between 5000°-7000°C). The pressure in the inner core is so high that even after having a high temperature, the inner core is in solid state and is not molten. The metals inside the cores are constantly moving which help the cores to rotate regularly. It is also believed that the inner core rotates faster than the entire planet.

17. Tectonic Plates

The lithosphere is broken up into many small sections/areas called crustal plates or tectonic plates. These tectonic plates fit into one another like jigsaw puzzle blocks. These plates are in constant motion but the movement is very slow that is about 3 cm per year. The motion of these tectonic plates is responsible for the change in the shape of continents and oceans. These plates are divided into two types: minor plates and major plates. If the boundaries of these plates bump up against one another while the movement, it can cause an earthquake.

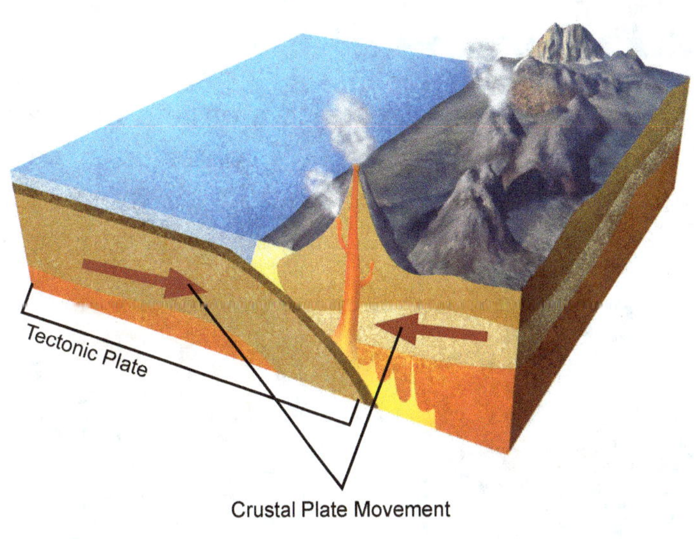

The San Andreas fault in California is a transform plate boundary separating the Pacific plate and North American plate.

18. Major and Minor Tectonic Plates

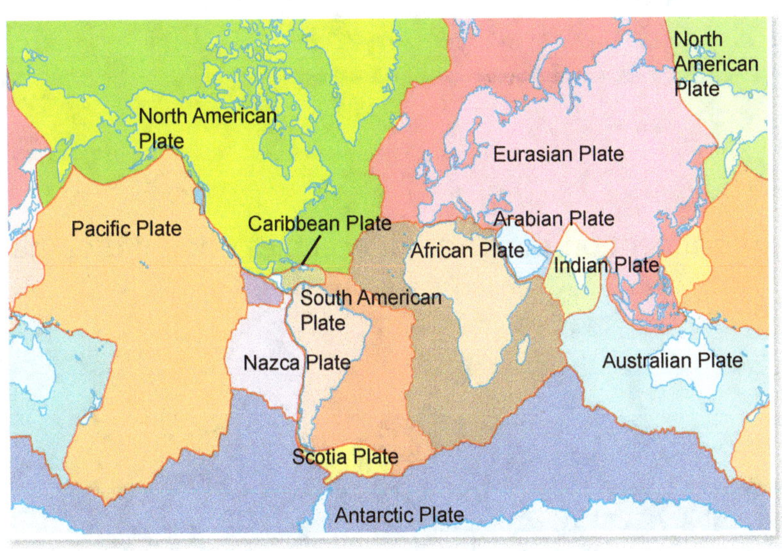

The Earth's surface (the crust) is divided into seven major and several minor tectonic plates. The seven major tectonic plates are– North American Plate, South American Plate, Eurasian Plate, African Plate, Antarctic plate, Australian-Indian plate and Pacific plate. Minor plates also play an important role when it comes to the shaping the Earth. Some of the minor plates are: the Arabian, Caribbean, Nazca and Scotia plates. These minor and major tectonic plates provide a framework for understanding the composition, structure and internal processes of the Earth.

19. Plate Boundaries

The lines where the tectonic plates meet are called the plate boundaries. There are three types of plate boundaries: divergent, convergent and transform. Divergent boundaries occur when the tectonic plates move apart. The convergent boundaries form when the tectonic plates move towards one another. The transform boundaries form when the tectonic plates move sideways in relation to one another at boundary.

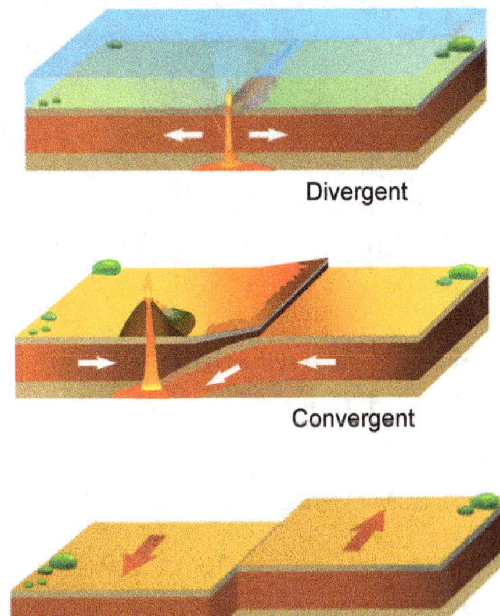

20. Continents

Continents are large pieces of land on the Earth that are separated by oceans, seas, rivers and mountains. The formation of continents began in the early Mesozoic era. About 270 million years ago, most of the dry land on the Earth was joined together. It was known as the 'supercontinent'. The giant ocean surrounding this supercontinent is known as Panthalassa. The evolution of the Earth surface and movement of tectonic plates broke up this giant landmass and gave rise to present-day continents. There are seven continents on the Earth: Asia, Africa, North America, South America, Antarctica, Europe and Australia.

Pangaea

Laurasia and Gondwana

Present-day Earth

Continental Drift

The theory that the continents were joined earlier and have drifted apart was first proposed by a German Scientist: Alfred Wegener in 1912.

21. Asia

Asia is the largest, most populated and diverse continent on the Earth. It occupies one-third of the land surface of the Earth.

Surface area: 44,579,000 km^2

Location: Extends in both Northern and Southern hemispheres

Major countries: China, Russia, India, Kazakhistan, Korea and Japan

Important physical features:

♦ Mount Everest (elevation above sea level 29,035 feet)

♦ The lowest point on the Earth's surface: The Dead Sea (depth: about 1,312 feet below sea level)

Major languages: Arabic, Mandarin, Hindi and Russian

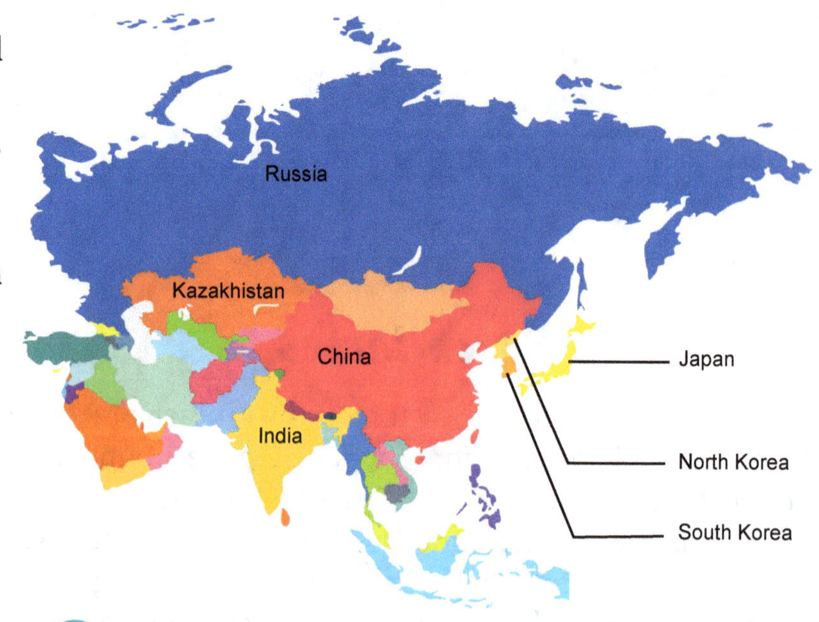

Hemisphere: Any circle drawn around the Earth that divides it into two equal halves is called hemisphere. There are four hemispheres: Northern, Southern, Eastern and Western.

22. Africa

Africa is the second largest continent on the Earth. Africa has a diverse range of mineral resources, including some of the world's largest reserves of fossil fuels, metallic ores and gems and precious metals.

Surface area: 30,365,000 km²

Location: Surrounds the equatorial line and the Eastern hemisphere

Major countries: Algeria, Congo, Kenya, Namibia, Sudan and South Africa

Important physical features:

- The highest point of Africa is Mount Kilimanjaro (elevation above sea level: 19,341 feet)
- World's largest desert: The Great Sahara desert (area: 9,065,000 km²)
- The East African Rift System and diverse wildlife in the vast forests
- Mountains: Atlas mountain range in northwestern Africa
- Rivers: Nile, Congo Niger

Major languages: Yoruba, Hausa and Swahili

23. North America

North America is the third largest continent on the Earth. It has some of the oldest rocks on the Earth. The Panama Canal, located in Central America, connects the Atlantic and the Pacific Ocean.

Surface area: 24,256,000 km²

Location: It is located in the Northern and Western hemispheres, between the Pacific and Atlantic Oceans

Major countries: Canada, Mexico, United States of America, West Indies and Alaska

Important physical features:

- Appalachian and Rocky Mountains to the east
- The St. Lawrence River separates parts of the United States from eastern Canada
- Highest point in North America: Mount McKinley in Alaska (elevation above sea level: 20,320 feet)

Major languages: French, Spanish and English

Largest island on the Earth: Greenland

24. South America

South America is the fourth largest continent on the Earth. It lies between the Atlantic and Pacific Oceans. It has the world's largest forest area. This continent looks like a triangle on the world map.

Surface area: 17,819,000 km²

Location: Western hemisphere, south of Central America

Major countries: Argentina, Chile, Columbia, Peru, Bolivia, Brazil and Venezuela

Important physical features:

- The Andes Mountains: vast series of high plateaus, spread from the southernmost tip to the Caribbean in north

- The Amazon Rainforest, the world's largest tropical rainforest in Brazil

- The Amazon River, the second longest river in the world

Major languages: Portuguese and Spanish

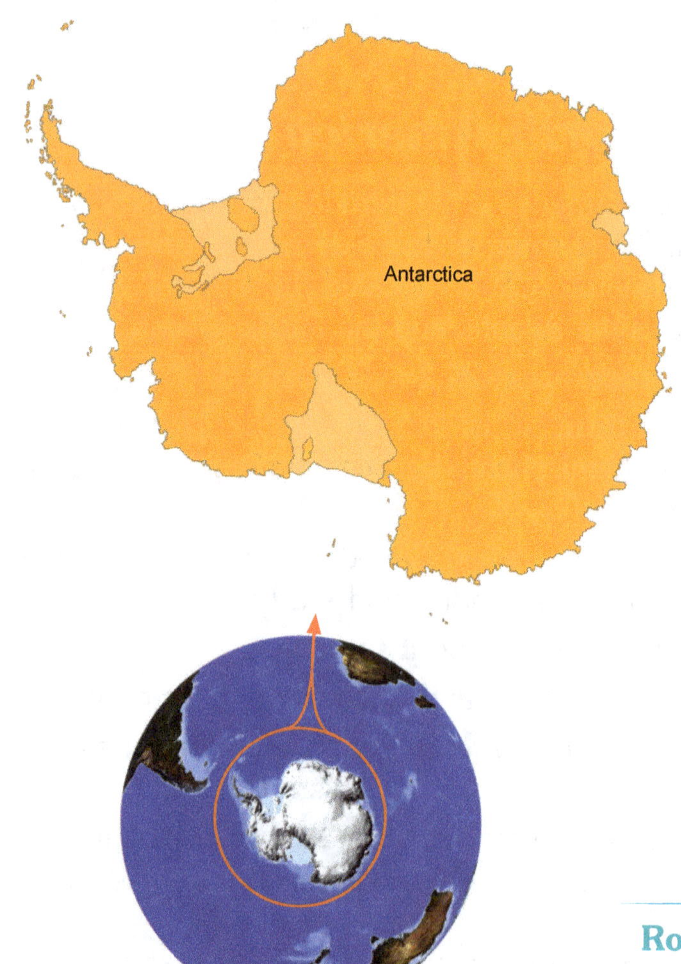

25. Antarctica

Antarctica is the fifth largest continent on the Earth. About 98-99% of the landmass of this continent is covered with an ice sheet. It is the coldest, driest and the windiest continent on the Earth. Only a few species of plants and animals that can adapt to their environment can survive here. No nation owns the land, so there are no countries in Antarctica. Only, a few countries, for example, the Unites States, operate science research stations here. Antarctica was first explored by Scott, a British National, during 1901-04.

Surface area: 13,209,000 km²

Location: Southern hemisphere, world's southernmost continent on the South Pole

Major countries: This continent is not divided into countries

Important physical features: Frozen land and glaciers

26. Europe

Europe is the second smallest continent on Earth. Europe and Asia share the same landmass. But because this landmass is so large, geographers have separated this huge landmass into two continents.

Surface area: 9,938,000 km²

Location: Northern hemisphere

Major countries: Norway, Sweden, Finland, Russia, Germany, Poland, Spain, France, Italy, Turkey, Hungary and Bulgaria

Important physical features:

- Mountains: The Alps, Pyrenees, Apennines and Balkans, helped to create defensible borders between areas
- Rivers: Danube, Rhine, Rhone, Loire, Elbe, Vistula and Volga
- Seas: Mediterranean, Baltic, North, and Black Seas

Major languages: Danish, Dutch, English, German, Swedish, French, Italian, Portuguese and Romanian

Eurasia is the combined name of two continents, Europe and Asia. Sometimes, they are referred as a single continent 'Eurasia'.

27. Australia

Australia is the smallest continent on the Earth. It is the only country that is wholly a continent. It is surrounded by the Indian and Pacific Oceans. Arafura and Timor Seas separate Australia from Asian continent. Its central area is mainly desert. Australia is known as the last of lands because it was the last continent to be explored by the Europeans, besides Antarctica.

Surface area: 7,687,000 km²

Location: Southern hemisphere

Major countries: Australia

Important physical features:

- World's largest coral reef–the Great Barrier Reef
- Huge wildlife, with several rare species of animals including kangaroos

Major language: English

28. Earth's Atmosphere

Planet Earth is surrounded by a thick blanket of air, called the atmosphere. This atmosphere is composed of about 20 different gases, but oxygen and nitrogen account for about 90% in dry air. The atmosphere was formed when the hot surface of the Earth began to cool. As the molten rocky mass of the newly formed Earth cooled, the most volatile and lightest substances evaporated away as gases from the Earth's interior. These gases formed the atmosphere. Sunlight and plants were mainly responsible for the changes in the composition of gases in the Earth's atmosphere.

29. Exosphere

The Earth's atmosphere is divided into five layers. The exosphere is the outermost layer of the Earth's atmosphere. The upper part of this layer merges with space; hence it has no definite outer limit. This layer has almost no air/gases. It starts around 500 km above the sea level and extends outwards and interacts with the solar winds. Many man-made satellites orbit the Earth within this layer. The temperature range remains constant that is around 1227 °C and the altitude does not create any difference. Whenever solar storms occur, the exospheric layer is compressed due to excessive heat and pressure.

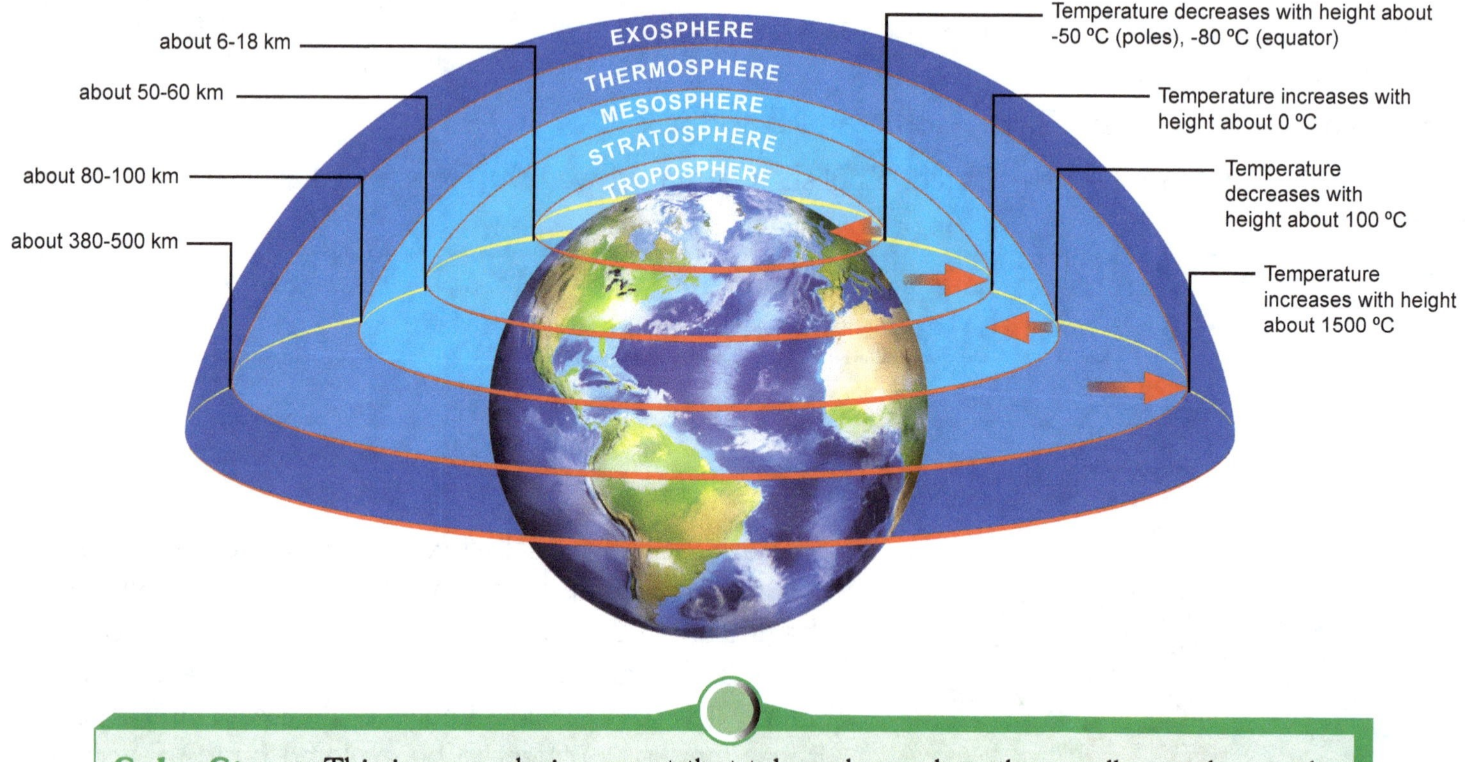

Solar Storm: This is an explosive event that takes place when the small particles on the surface of the sun collide and produce a huge flash of light.

30. Thermosphere

The thermosphere is also called the 'upper atmosphere'. This layer of the Earth's atmosphere lies between the exosphere and the mesosphere. It starts at 80 km above the sea level, and extends up to 450 km above the sea level. The temperature in this layer increases with the increase in altitude. The thermosphere is a thin layer due to which it holds very little heat. The lower part of the thermosphere contains ionised molecules which reflect low frequency radio waves back to the Earth and is called the ionosphere.

31. Ionosphere

It is an ion (small charged particles) rich layer that includes the lower part of the thermosphere and some part of the mesosphere. The ions in this layer affect the radio waves and are responsible for the creation of the electrical layer. This layer is very important for reflecting the radio waves and helping the communication satellites that orbit in space. The upper region of the ionosphere is called the magnetosphere as the charged particles present in this layer affect the magnetic field of the Earth. The ionosphere and the magnetosphere were discovered by a German mathematician Carl Friedrich Gauss in 1839.

33. Stratosphere

The stratosphere lies between the troposphere and the mesosphere. It is the second layer of the atmosphere as we go upward. The highest clouds are generally found in this layer. This layer of the atmosphere extends from the boundary of the troposphere at about 10-17 km to 50 km above the sea level. The atmosphere is more dry and dense in this layer. The lower portion of this layer has constant temperature, but as we travel further above in this layer, the temperature rises with respect to the altitude. The ozone layer lies in the upper region of the stratosphere. Jet planes fly in the stratosphere.

34. Troposphere

The troposphere is the closest and lowest layer of the Earth's atmosphere. It is the layer where all weather changes take place and cloud formation occurs. The troposphere lies between the Earth (lithosphere) and the stratosphere (10-18 km above the sea level). This layer makes about 70-80% of the total atmosphere. This layer carries the densest composition of gases and atmospheric molecules. As we move above in the troposphere from the Earth, the temperature decreases. This feature of decreasing temperature differentiates the troposphere from the stratosphere. The abundance of oxygen in this layer supports life.

32. Mesosphere

The mesosphere lies just above the stratosphere. It is the upper atmosphere region, which is located between 50 km and 80 km above the sea level. The mesosphere is the coldest layer of the atmosphere. The temperature decreases with the increase in altitude. The mesosphere is thicker than the exosphere and the thermosphere. The mesosphere and the stratosphere together are often called the 'middle atmosphere'. Meteors that enter the Earth's atmosphere, face friction in this layer. Due to this friction, these meteors end up burning themselves.

Ozone Layer: It is the protective layer blanketing the Earth and protecting it from the harmful UV rays.

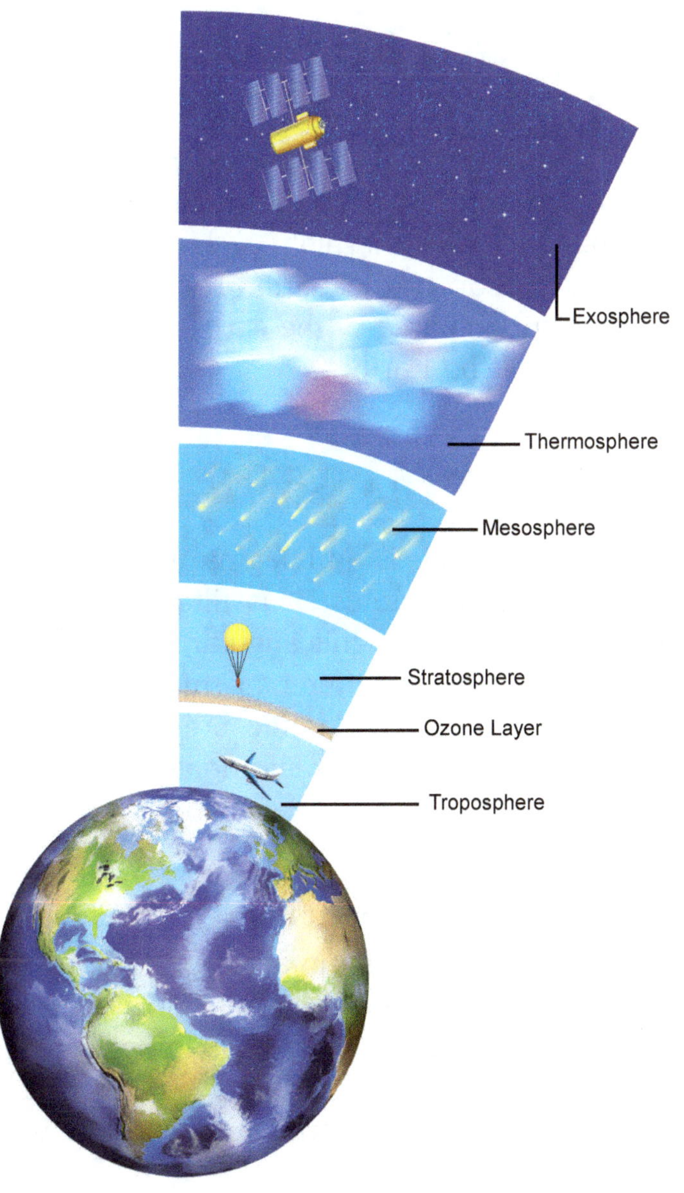

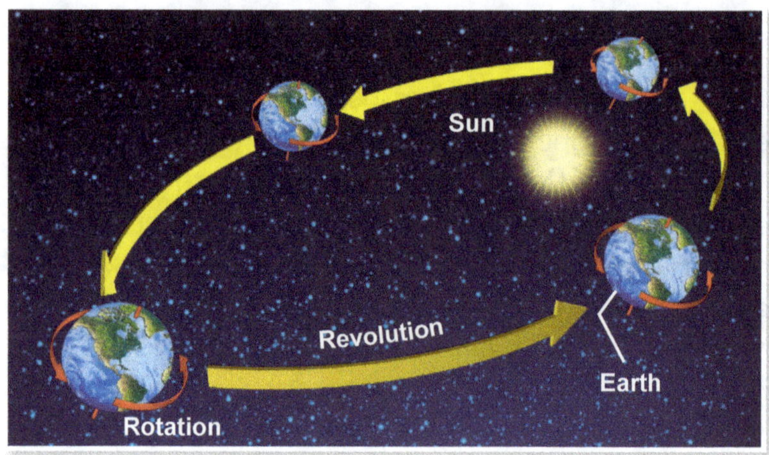

35. Earth's Movement

The Earth is not a static body. It continuously revolves around the Sun in an elliptical path. Its movement affects our daily life, crucially. Two important movements of the Earth that affect our life are: rotation of the Earth around its axis and revolution of the Earth around the Sun. It takes the Earth about 24 hours to finish one complete rotation and around 365.25 days to complete one revolution. The principle of day-night, the occurrence of various seasons, and the appearance of various shapes of moon depends on the Earth's movement.

The Earth rotates fastest at the equator. The speed of the rotation goes on decreasing as the distance from the equator increases.

36. Earth's Rotation

The Earth rotates around an imaginary line, called the axis. This axis runs through the North and the South Pole. If the rotating Earth is viewed from the North Pole, it seems rotating from west to east that is counter-clockwise. Due to this movement or rotation of the Earth from west to east, we experience day and night cycle. This whole cycle of day and night takes 24 hours, and is called the daily motion of the Earth. The Earth rotates at about 1600 km per hour at the equator. But since the surface area of the earth is so vast with diverse topography, we do not feel the rotational movement of the Earth.

37. Tilt of the Earth's Axis

The Earth's axis is an imaginary line around which the Earth rotates. It is tilted at a fixed angle of 23.5°. Due to this angular tilt, the Earth faces the Sun in a differential manner. Or in other words, this tilt helps the Sun to shine on different latitudes at different angles throughout the year.

Day and Night Formation

The Earth is tilted at an angle of 23.5°. The sun rays fall on the surface of the earth, but due to the spherical shape only half of the globe receives the sunlight. The portion which receives the sunlight experiences day whereas the opposite side has night. This division is defined as the circle of illumination. As the Earth rotates on its axis and revolves around the sun, the face that had night slowly gets the sunlight and experiences day. This period of rotation is called Earth day and the duration is 24 hours.

38. Revolution of the Earth

Revolution is the movement of the Earth around the Sun in its orbit. The revolution is commonly known as the annual cycle of the Earth. The revolution of the Earth takes place from west to east, same as the rotation. The Earth takes 365.25 days to complete one revolution and this period is referred as one year. The pathway on which the Earth travels around the Sun, the orbit is elliptical. This elliptical shape is responsible for changing distance between the Sun and the Earth. It is also responsible for the change in the season. When the Earth is at the farthest point on the ellipse of the orbit, the part of the Earth facing away from the Sun, experiences winter season.

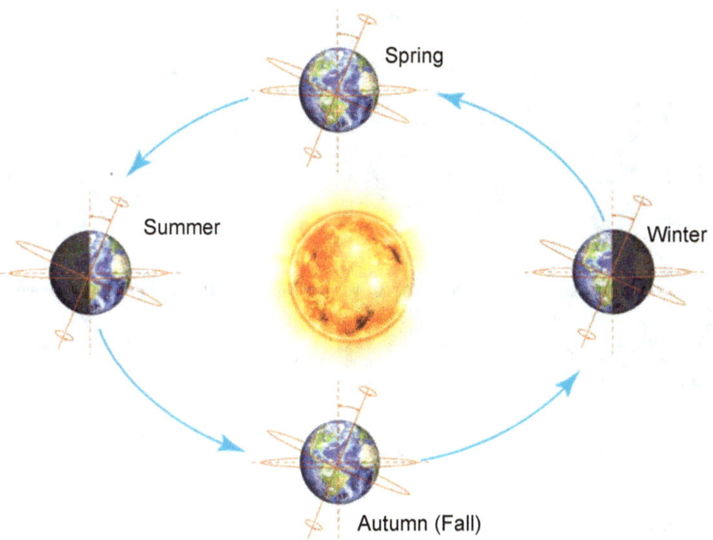

Seasons – Movement of the Earth around the Sun

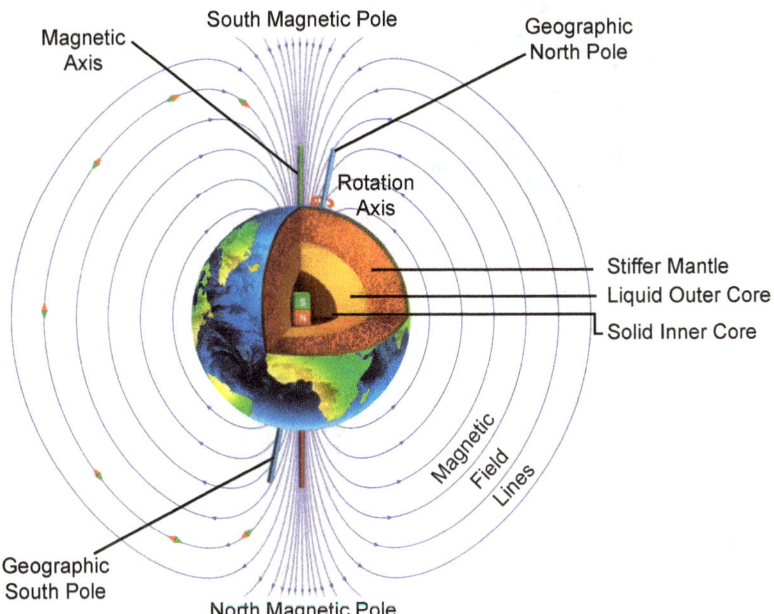

39. Earth's Magnetic Field

The Earth's magnetic field is also known as 'the geomagnetic field'. Since past, our ancestors have used magnetic compasses to find their way around the Earth. Magnetic compasses have a needle made up of magnet that lines up with the Earth's magnetic field, which is aligned north-south wherever you are on the Earth. This geomagnetic field is created by the strong electric currents within the core. The Earth's magnetic field was studied by a German mathematician and astronomer Carl Friedrich Gauss in 1830. He deduced that the Earth's magnetic field is the result of the principal dipolar components which are present inside the Earth's surface.

The outer core of the Earth is liquid. The magnetic field is the result of the movement of this core. The Earth's magnetic field is like a big magnet.

40. Earth Year

The Earth rotates on its axis around the Sun in the same direction or a fixed orbit. It takes 365.25 days to complete this journey. These 365.25 days are counted as one year, which is also called an 'Earth year'. The distance covered by the Earth in one Earth year is about 960,000,000 km. The Earth travels about 105,600 km per day.

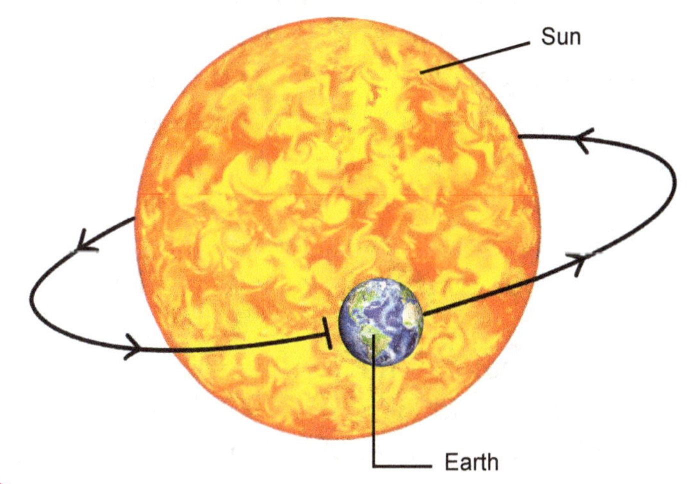

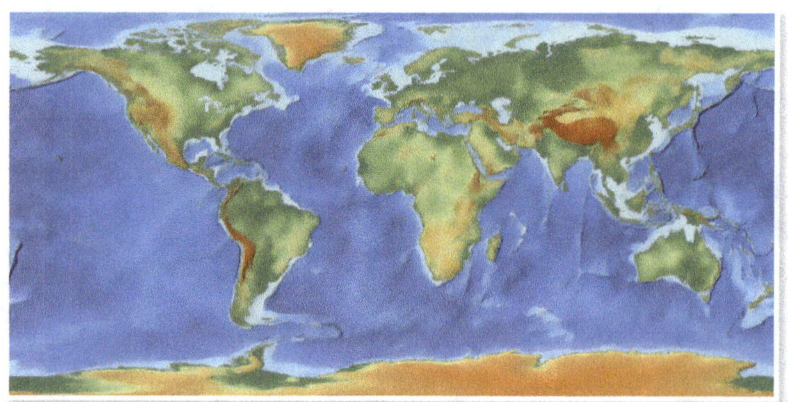

41. Earth's Topography

Topography is the study of the shape and features of the Earth's surface. Variations in the climate in different regions of the Earth are a part of topography. Distance of a place from the equator decides the climate of that particular region. This difference in location and related differential climate results in a variable ecosystem on the planet. Other crucial topographic features include: mountains, plateaus, plains, rivers, lakes, waterfall, seas, oceans, etc. Topography includes study about the latitude, longitude, equator, hemispheres, and South and North Poles.

42. Equator

The equator is an imaginary line around the middle of planet Earth. It divides the Earth into two hemispheres, the Northern hemisphere and the Southern hemisphere. It forms the imaginary reference line on the Earth's surface from which latitude is calculated. So, the equator is the line of 0° latitude. The Earth's circumference is maximum at the equator that is about 40,075 km. The temperatures in locations on or around the equator are usually high all around the year. The Earth's equatorial region is mostly covered with water.

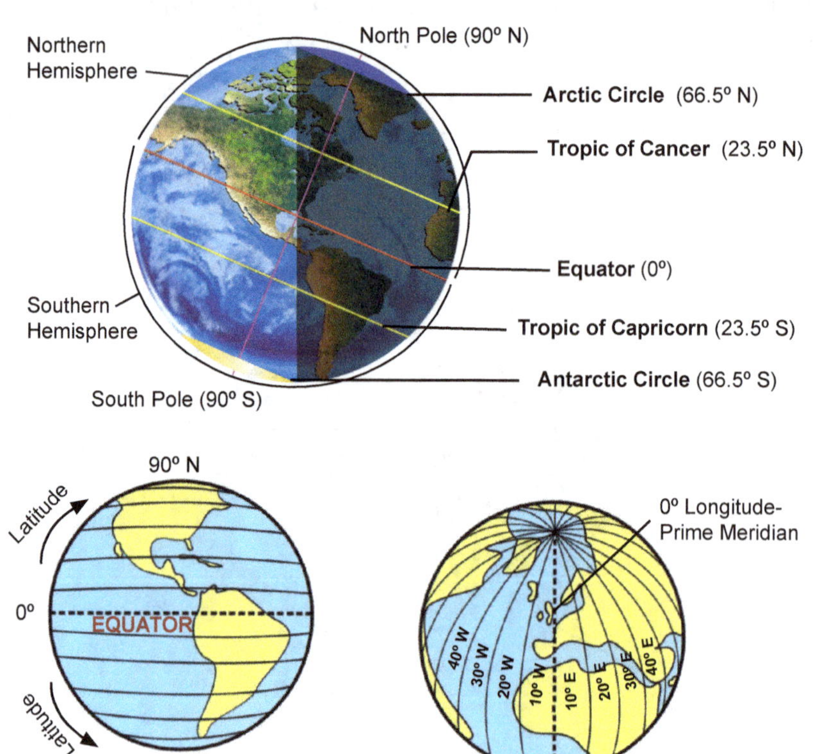

43. Latitude

There are several imaginary lines parallel to the equator. Latitude measures north or south of the Earth's equator. The latitude circles the Earth in an east-west direction. These lines help to locate places on the Earth. These lines are known as parallels. A circle of latitude is an imaginary ring linking all points sharing a parallel. The parallel is measured in terms of degrees from the equator. The equator is at 0° latitude. The North Pole is at 90°N latitude and the South Pole is at 90°S latitude.

44. Longitude

Longitudinal lines are the vertical lines running around the Earth, meeting the North and the South Pole. These vertical lines measure east or west of the prime meridian by imaginary lines. The central point, where the longitude is 0°, is called the prime meridian which is a line travelling through Greenwich, England, from the North Pole to the South Pole. It divides the sphere into two equal parts, the eastern and the western hemisphere. These vertical lines are known as meridians. Each meridian is measured as one arc degree. The farthest point in the East measures 180°E and the farthest point on the west measures 180°W.

45. Hemispheres

Hemispheres are the equal half portion of the Earth. When we separate the Earth half way between the North and South Poles, at the equator, we can locate the Northern and the Southern hemisphere. The half fragment of the Earth, centred on the North Pole, is the Northern hemisphere and the fragment of the Earth centred on the South Pole is the Southern hemisphere. The Eastern and the Western hemisphere are located on either side of the prime meridian.

46. North Pole

The North Pole is the northernmost point of the Earth's axis that lies in the middle of the Arctic Ocean. At the North Pole, all directions point south. The location of the North Pole in terms of latitude is 90°N. All the longitudinal lines or the meridians meet at the North Pole as well as the South Pole. In comparison to the South Pole, the North Pole is much warmer. This is because the elevation of the North Pole with respect to the sea level is low and it is located in the middle of an ocean. The North Pole receives sunlight in a very specific pattern. It experiences only one sunrise (in March) and one sunset (in September). In summers, the Sun never sets and in winters the Sun never rises.

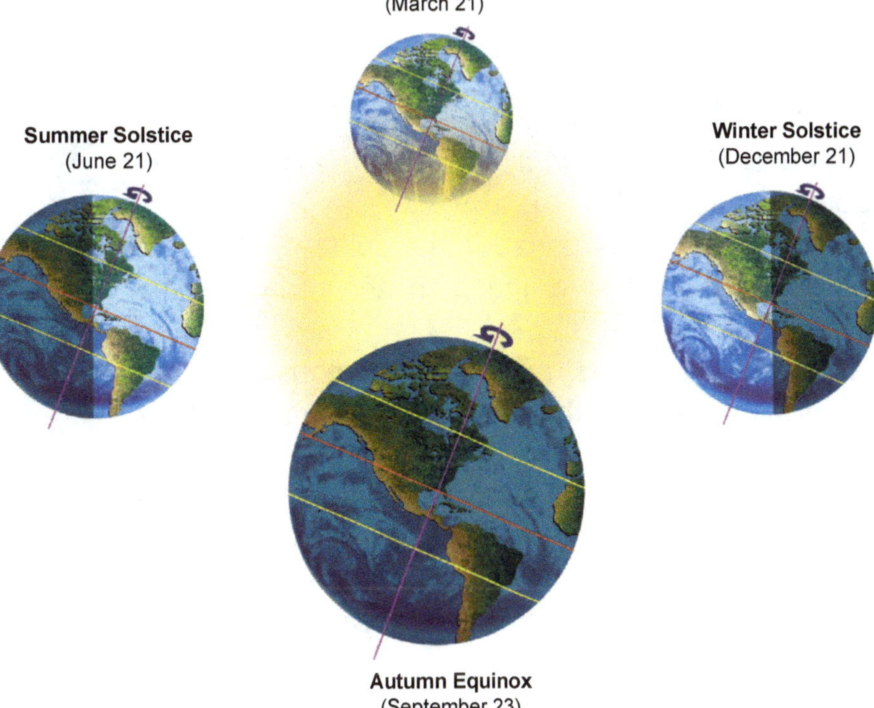

Equinox: It is that day of the year when the length of the day is equal to the length of the night. There are two equinoxes in a year: one is around March 21 and another is around September 22.

47. South Pole

The South Pole is the southernmost point of the Earth's axis that lies on the ice-covered continent of Antarctica. At the South Pole, all directions point north. The latitude of the South Pole is 90°S South. And like North Pole all lines of the longitude meet here too. The South Pole is the coldest place on the Earth since it is surrounded by a thick ice-sheeted continent. Unlike the North Pole, the South Pole experiences its sunrise in the month of September equinox and sunset in the month of March equinox every year.

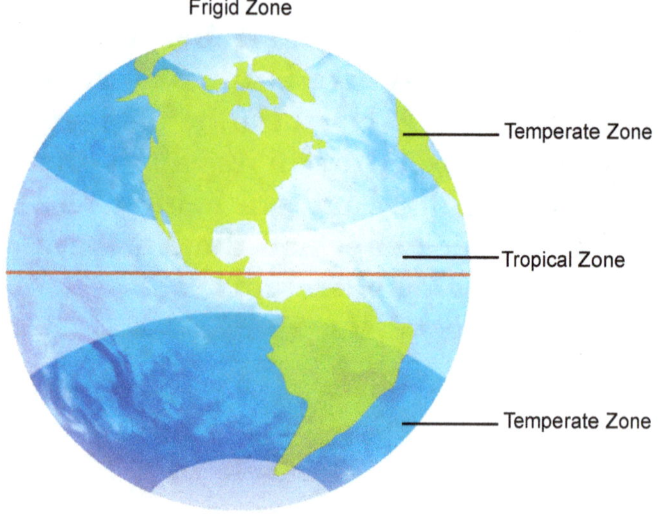

48. Climatic Zone

Climate is a term which relates the weather condition of a region with the respective temperature. The Earth experiences different climates throughout the year. The topography of the Earth is very much responsible for variable climates across the planet. The climate also varies due to the interaction of sunlight with the atmosphere, along with the various landforms such as mountains, plains, seas and oceans. The major factors that affect the climate are: latitude, distance from sea, and elevation above the sea level. Some regions on the Earth are very hot, some very cool, while some moderate.

49. Polar Region

Temperature: The temperature in the polar region is approximately –30°C to –139°C.

Climate: Polar regions are the coldest regions of the world that have permanently frozen surface under thick snow.

Location on Earth: The polar regions surround the North and the South Pole that is the Arctic and the Antarctic region.

Flora and Fauna: Due to frozen soil, no species of plants can be seen here. However, a few species of animals are found in the polar region; these are squirrel, wolf, fox, reindeer, penguin, polar bear, walrus, seal and whale.

50. Tundra

Temperature: The temperature is approximately 17°C to –30°C, sub-freezing to moderately low precipitation.

Climate: The climate is very harsh during winters with strong winds; however, summers are cool and pleasant.

Location on Earth: Along the coast of the Arctic Ocean.

Flora and Fauna: Due to frozen soil, no species of plants can be seen here. But a few fungi, such as lichen and moss, are found. The main species of animals found in tundra climate are polar bear, musk ox, Arctic fox, snow owl, reindeer and lemming.

51. Temperate Zone

Temperature: Approximately –6°C to 25°C.

Climate: Temperate zone receives rainfall throughout the year and the temperature varies with seasons.

Location on Earth: Between the equator and the North and South Poles this region is closer to the North and the South Pole.

Flora and Fauna: Deciduous forests found in regions of the Northern hemisphere are warm and the grasslands are mostly devoid of big trees. Arboreal mammals like greater glider, bat and koala are common in most regions of temperate forest.

52. Tropical Zone

Temperature: Approximately 20°C to 30°C.

Climate: The climate is generally warm with two main seasons: wet season and dry season.

Location on the Earth: This covers the land around and on either side of the equator.

Flora and Fauna: Lush green forests and dense growth of bushes and trees form tropical forests. A variety of animals, like monkeys, chimpanzees, leopards, hyenas, elephants, hippocampus, jaguars, lions, rhinoceroses, etc. can be found.

53. Mediterranean Zone

Temperature: Approximately 10°C to 22.0°C.

Climate: Hot, dry summers and cool, wet winters; heavily influenced by current of air which moves between the land and the sea.

Location on the Earth: Located between 30° and 45° latitude north and south of the equator and on the western sides of the continents.

Flora and Fauna: Scrubby, dense vegetation composed of broad-leaved evergreen shrubs, bushes and small trees usually less than 2.5m tall, especially citrus fruits with thick skins.

54. Continental Zone

Temperature: Approximately 0°C to 40°C.

Climate: Extreme hot summers and extreme cold winters, with moderate rainfall. Rains in summers and snow in winters at some places.

Location on the Earth: Located away from the oceans in the middle of the continents.

Flora and Fauna: Only a few trees like willow are found on the banks of the rivers. Apart from it, wheat and tall grasses are also found. It is well-known for a large number of animals like coyote, fox, rabbit, wolf, hawk, horse, owl, etc.

55. Equatorial Zone

Temperature: Approximately 17°C to 30°C, consistently high temperature.

Climate: Constantly hot and wet climate with plentiful precipitation with heavy cloud cover, and high humidity, with very little annual temperature variation.

Location on the Earth: Lies within 12° latitude of the equator.

Flora and Fauna: Broad-leaved trees, huge number of plants. Large mammals and small birds, insects and reptiles. The equatorial region is also called the tropical rainforest. It is an area of tall, mostly evergreen trees and a high amount of rainfall.

Forests surrounding the Amazon River in South America and the Congo River in Africa are the largest rainforests.

56. Desert

Temperature: Approximately 21°C to 48°C.

Climate: Very hot climate in day time; daily temperature variations are extreme.

Location on the Earth: Deserts are found in every continent and cover about one-fifth of Earth's land area.

Flora and Fauna: Saguaro cacti that grow in the Sonoran Desert of Arizona and northern Mexico expand like accordions to store water in the cells of their trunks and branches. Other desert plants have very deep roots, like mesquite.

57. Weather

Weather is condition of the surrounding atmosphere at a particular time. It is described as a combination of various factors such as, temperature, moisture and air flow. However, the most crucial factor is heating and cooling of air through the Sun. Weather affects our life in many ways. For example, the type of shelter we choose, the food we eat and the clothes we wear. Weather is an unstable factor. For example, we may experience a windy evening after a sunny morning. Sometimes weather is referred as today's climate.

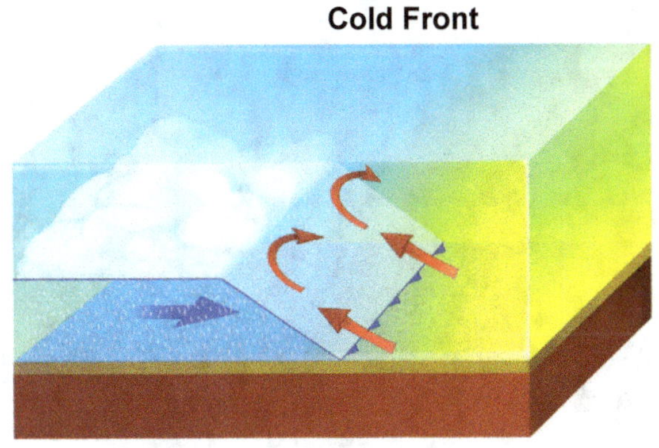
Cold Front

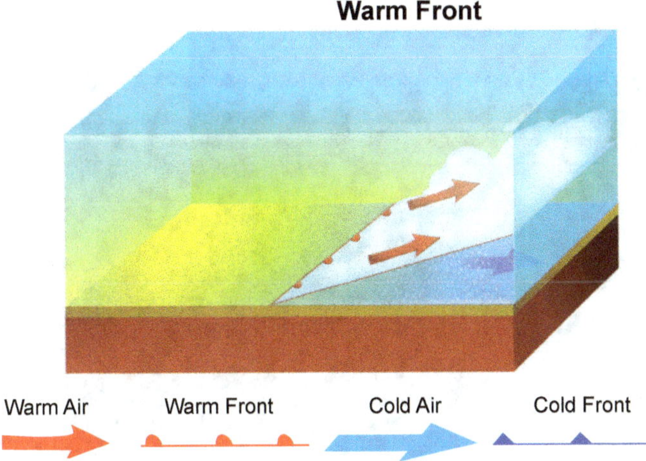
Warm Front

58. Weather Fronts

A weather front is a zone or boundary of transition where two different types of air masses meet. For example, a warm air mass and a cold air mass. The drastic changes in the weather occur due to these weather fronts.

There are three types of fronts: cold, warm and stationary.

- A cold front is a boundary between rapidly moving cold air and warm air mass. The cold air replaces the warm air with a push.

- A warm front is a boundary between slowly moving warm air and a mass of cold air. Here the warm air replaces cooler air.

- A stationary front shows little or no drastic movement in between two contrasting air masses.

59. Wind

The moving air in the atmosphere is called wind. The movement of air is caused due to the changes in temperature. When the temperature of air increases, it expands. This expansion makes the air lighter and the air rises. As the warm air rises, the empty place is filled by cooler air. This continuous movement of air is wind. The larger the differences in temperature, the more varying the wind speeds are. Mostly the wind flow originates from the equator to the Poles as the equator receives maximum heat.

60. Wind Direction

The direction in which the wind blows is called wind direction. For example, wind blowing from east to west is called easterly wind, while that blowing from west to east is westerly wind. The direction in which the wind flows affects the climate on daily basis. For example, if the wind blows from a warm place, it will be hot and if it blows from a cold place, it will be cool. The direction of the wind is measured with respect to the compass reading, which is in terms of 360° on the compass (North). The common types of wind observed across the planet are: polar high, polar easterlies, polar front, westerlies, horse latitudes, trade winds and doldrums.

61. Sea Breeze

The surface of the Earth warms up more quickly in the morning than the surface of the water. This is the reason the air above the beach becomes warmer and thinner creating low-air pressure. While the air above the sea is cooler and denser, creating high pressure. This difference in the air pressures creates the movement of the wind from high-pressure areas to low-pressure areas. Hence, cool air moves from the sea towards the land. This is called sea breeze, which blows during the day.

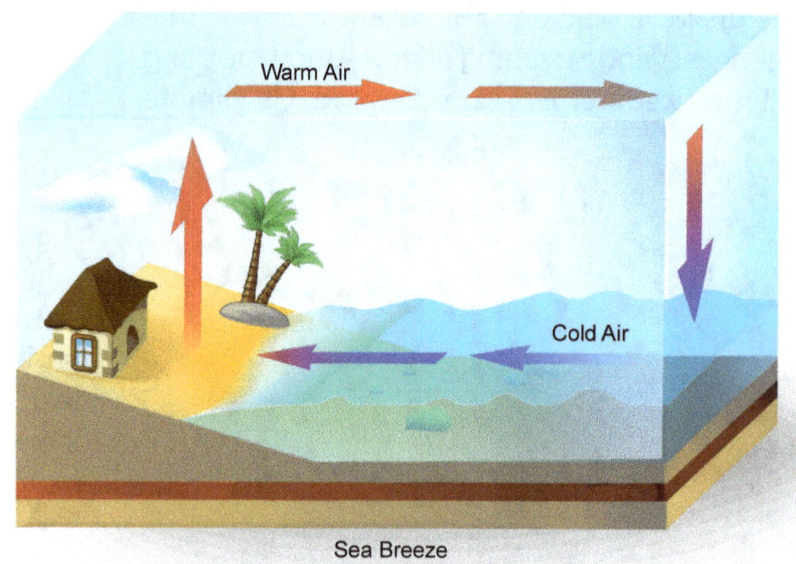

- Warm air expands because the molecules present in warm air move apart on heating. This makes the air lighter and a low pressure zone is created.
- Cool air is heavy and compressed because the molecules present in the cool air are close to one another. And due to this, a high-pressure zone is created in cool air regions.

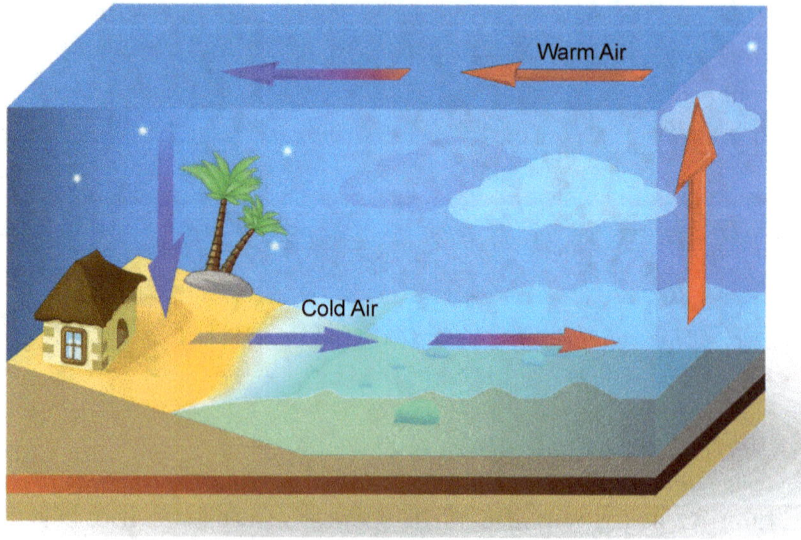

62. Land Breeze

The Earth's surface cools faster than the sea after the Sun has set. As we know, the cool air is dense and has high-pressure, so the rapidly cooling Earth's surface will have higher air-pressure over it than the sea. As a result, the movement of the air begins from a high-pressure area (Earth's surface or land) to a low-pressure area (sea). This is called the land breeze, which blows during the night. This whole phenomenon of the sea and land breeze occurs in the coastal area.

63. Water Cycle

Water cycle is the continuous movement of water in the atmosphere. Water present in ponds, lakes, rivers, seas and oceans changes its form and converts to water vapour due to the heat of the atmosphere (evaporation). As the water vapour rises, the low temperature of atmosphere causes condensation of the water vapour. Tiny drops of water thus formed join together to form clouds. The lighter clouds keep on growing in size. They are moved from one place to another with the help of air. When the clouds become too heavy, it becomes difficult for them to hold water, and this results in rain (precipitation). The rain water gets collected in the water bodies present on the Earth. This whole process of movement of water is called water cycle.

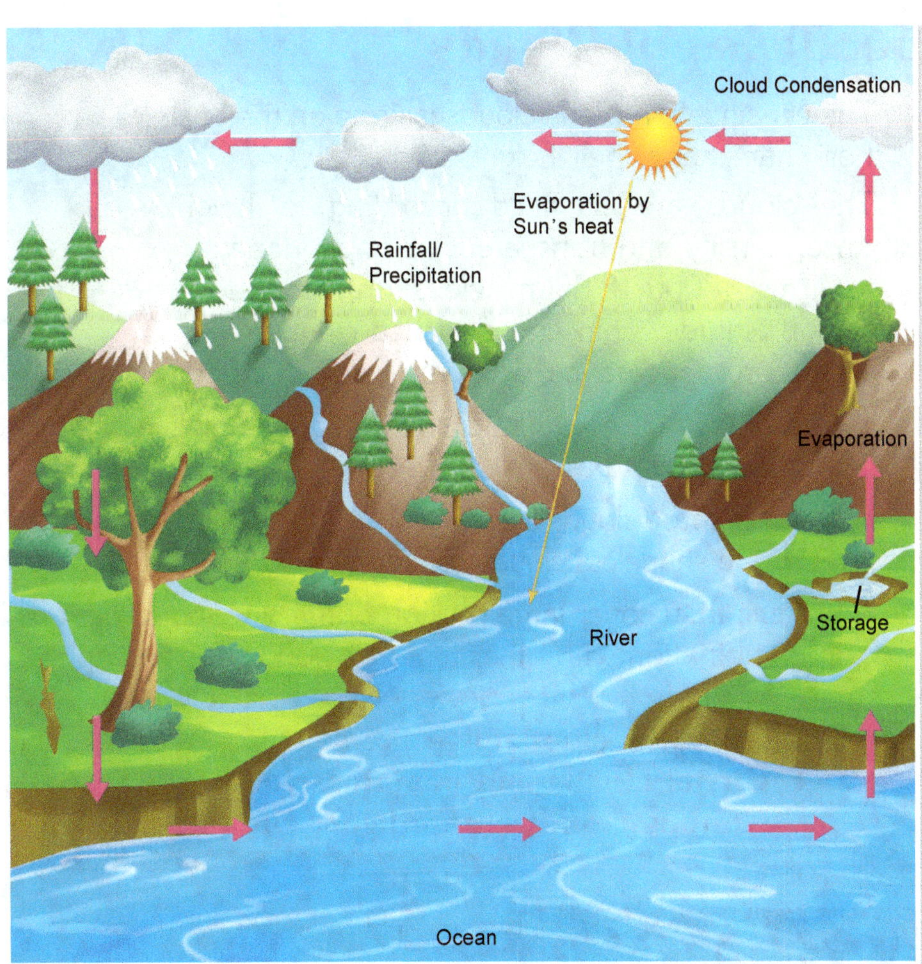

64. Humidity

The amount of moisture or water vapour present in air is called humidity. Humidity affects the climate of a place. The wind that blows from the sea towards the land brings a lot of moisture with it and makes the weather humid. The places near the sea are more humid than those far away from the sea. Humid weather makes us sweat considerably. Humidity is affected by the temperature of the atmosphere. The air that is warm can hold more moisture than the cooler one. Hence, tropics are more humid than the poles.

65. Clouds

Clouds are an important part of the water cycle. When the water on the Earth's surface gets warm, it gets evaporated and converted into water vapour. The warm air containing the vapour rises up in the atmosphere and slowly gets cooled. The cool air gets saturated with the vapour and loses its capacity to hold excess water vapour. The vapour thus condenses on the dust particles present in the atmosphere and forms water droplets. At times the temperature in the atmosphere is so low that these droplets convert into ice crystals. Eventually, these ice crystals cluster and float in the atmosphere due to their light weight. These floating visible masses of water droplets/ice crystals are clouds.

66. Types of Clouds

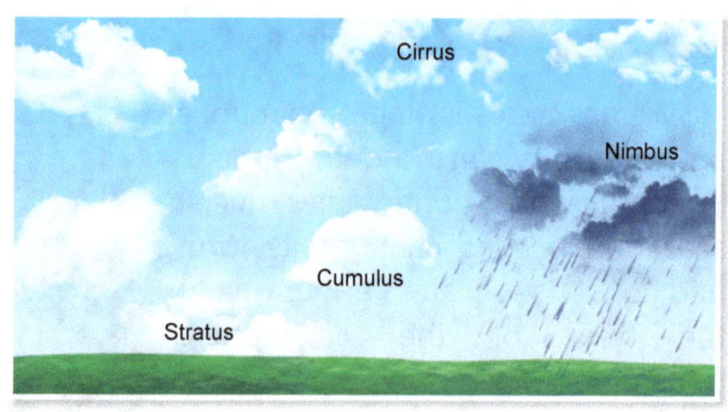

The classification of the clouds is done on the basis of their shapes and their heights in the sky.

The clouds are classified according to height, expanse, density and transparency or opaqueness.

- Cirrus (8000-12,000m elevation): formed at high altitude. Thin and detached clouds having feathery appearance. They are white in colour.
- Cumulus (4,000-7,000m elevation): they look like cotton wool. They are scattered here and there and have a flat base.
- Nimbus: these clouds are formed near the surface of the earth and are extremely dense and opaque. They are shapeless clouds. They are blackish to dark greyish in colour. These are rain clouds.
- Stratus: they cover large portion of the sky and appear as layers in the sky. They generally form in combination with other types of clouds, for example: Cirro-stratus, nimbo-stratus.

- **Cumulus clouds give the sign of upcoming rain.**
- **Cirrus clouds and cumulus clouds are responsible for good weather.**
- **Nimbus clouds create heavy thunderstorm with heavy rain.**

67. Rain

Rain means falling of water on the Earth from the clouds. It maintains the continuity of water cycle. It is an important weather component that affects the climate of a place. The region of the Earth that receives rainfall less than 254 mm per year is classified as desert. There are some regions on the Earth that receive rainfall less than 254 mm per year, but are not classified as deserts; they are Polar Regions and high mountains. On the contrary, there are some regions on the Earth that receive rainfall more than 2540 mm per year; they are classified as rainforests.

68. Snow

Snow is the solid form of water. It forms when the air is below freezing point and the water vapour present in the air solidifies. The snowflakes formed have very unique shape that is crystalline in nature. This crystalline shape is due to the chemical formulae of water that has two atoms of hydrogen and one of oxygen (H_2O). The size of the snowflakes is dependent on the temperature of the atmosphere. The colder the temperature, the smaller the snowflakes are.

69. Season

Season is a period when the weather condition remains constant with only slight variations. For example, in summer season, the weather remains hot with small variation in day-to-day temperature. In general, there are four seasons: summer, winter, rainy and autumn. Why do we have different seasons? The main reason behind this is:

- Revolution of Earth around the Sun in an elliptical orbit.
- And the tilt of Earth on its axis.

Due to the revolution and the tilt of the Earth, the sun rays fall variably on different regions of the Earth. The difference in the way the sun rays fall on the Earth's surface leads to occurrence of different seasons.

Hibernation: It is also known as winter sleep when animals living in extreme cold regions bury themselves in warm shelters.

Spring

Summer

Autumn

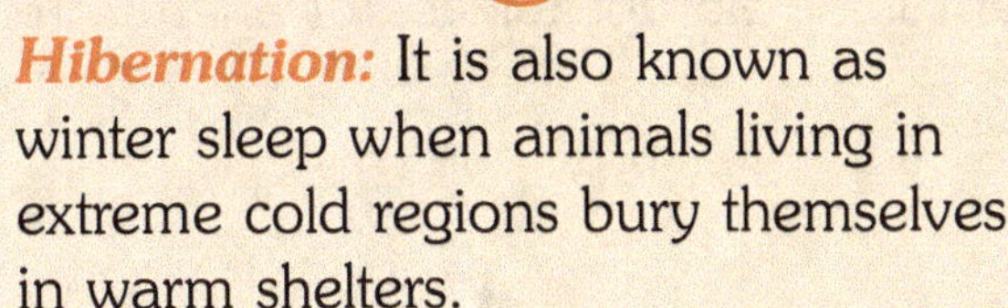
Winter

70. Summer and Winter

Summer is the season when we experience plenty of daylight, long days and short nights. In the Northern hemisphere June 22 is the longest day of summer whereas in the Southern hemisphere it is the shortest day of winter. When the Northern hemisphere is tilted towards the Sun and is closest to it, there is summer in the Northern hemisphere (June 22-September 23) and winter in the Southern hemisphere. However, when direct sun-rays fall on the Southern hemisphere (December 22-March 21), it experiences summer and the Northern hemisphere experiences winter.

71. Spring and Autumn

Spring and autumn seasons are the seasons when neither of the two hemispheres are tilted more towards the Sun. The temperature is moderate. The Northern hemisphere experiences spring between March 21-June 21 (the duration between winter and summer) and the Southern hemisphere experiences it between September 23-December 21 (the duration between summer and winter). Similarly, during the spring season trees are in blossom whereas during autumn leaves fall off trees. Spring is the season of festivals when most of the sowing of crops takes place. The birds migrate towards cooler areas before start of summers and hibernating animals come out of hibernation in the spring season. The autumn season is associated with the period of harvest. Animals gather food for the upcoming winter season.

72. Natural Disasters

Natural disasters are adverse events of Nature which cause huge damage to the lives of the people and the natural habitat. The reasons behind these events are the changes that happen deep inside the Earth and on its surface. Natural disasters are categorised into three major categories:

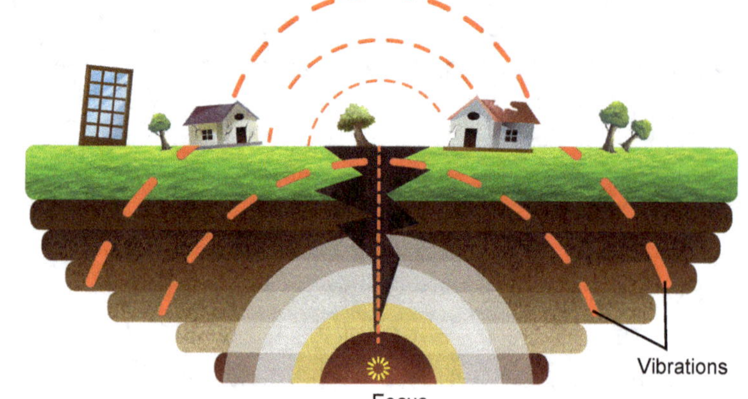

- Disasters caused by the movement of the Earth's surface and related tectonic plates: for example, earthquakes, volcanic eruptions, and tsunamis.

- Disasters related to weather: for example, snowstorm, avalanche, hurricanes, tornadoes, extreme heat and extreme cold.

- Disasters that arise as a consequence of extreme weather events: for example, flood, landslides, famine, forest fire, etc.

73. Earthquake

An earthquake is the sudden movement of the Earth's crust or vibration of Earth's surface. It starts at a specific point known as the focus and spreads circularly in all directions. These vibrations cause severe damages. The reason behind this unexpected movement is an abrupt release of energy that has travelled through the solid rocks from underground to the surface. The intensity or fastness of the earthquake is measured on the Richter Scale from 1 to 8. Small tremors, called 'aftershocks', may occur after a big earthquake.

Earthquakes generally take place at the following places:

- where mountain chains are being uplifted;
- where active volcanoes are present; and,
- near minor tectonic plates.

74. Seismic Waves

Seismic waves are the vibrations generated during an earthquake. There are three types of seismic waves:

P waves: These waves can travel through both the solid and liquid forms of the material in the Earth's interior. These waves have the ability to compress and stretch the rocks.

S waves: These waves can travel only through solid matter and are called the S or secondary waves. Speed of S wave is 2/3rd of the speed of the P wave.

L waves: These waves move only on the surface of the Earth; they are called the L or surface waves. These are the slowest waves but cause maximum damage at the epicentre.

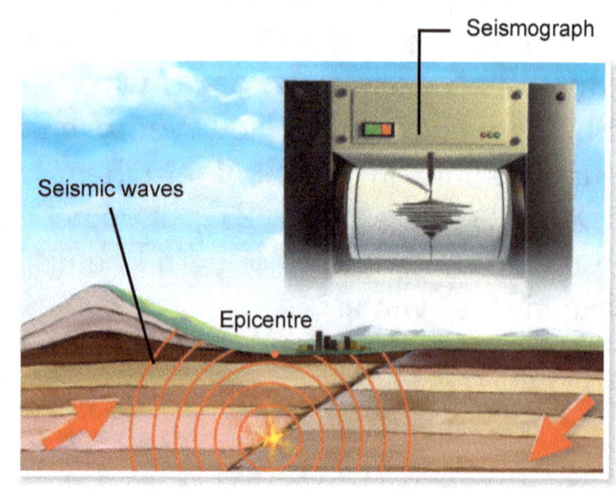

75. Volcano

A volcano is an opening on the Earth's crust from where molten rock, gases and pyroclastic debris erupt. Volcanoes erupt when the plates of the Earth's surface collide and one plate is pushed beneath another. This collision releases a lot of energy which melts the rocks, and the molten rocks rise and erupt as magma. The lava comes out through a vertical tunnel called a vent and fills a hollow called crater, at the top. The magma that reaches the Earth's surface is called lava. Cool, solidified lava forms rocks.

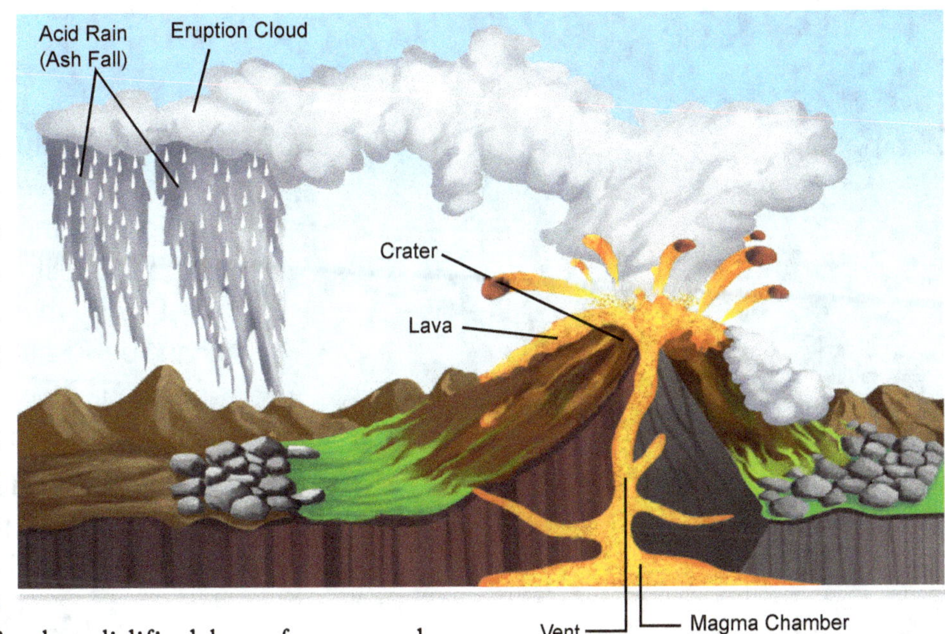

76. Volcanic Eruptions

Volcanoes can be classified according to the type of eruptions they exhibit. There are three main types of volcanoes on this basis: explosive, quiet and intermediate.

Explosive or Stratocone: The structure of this volcano is steep-sided. It gives out lots of gas, ash, pumice but less amount of lava. The lava which is released is stiff and the explosion mostly contains silica.

Quiet: These volcanoes have gentle slopes. They give out lots of lava with minor explosion. The lava is mainly basalt and is more fluid. Lava flows for a longer time.

Intermediate: They are a combination of explosive and quiet volcanoes. Mount Vesuvius of Naples in Italy is an intermediate type.

77. Tsunami

Tsunami means 'harbour wave' in Japanese language. This is caused by an underwater earthquake occurring less than 50 km below the seafloor. Tsunami occurs when one tectonic plate slips under another plate. This slip of plates leads to earthquake (Intensity: at least 5.5 on Richter scale). It can also occur due to coastal or underwater eruptions or landslide. The destructive force of tsunami can be felt thousands of kilometres away from the epicentre of the underwater earthquake.

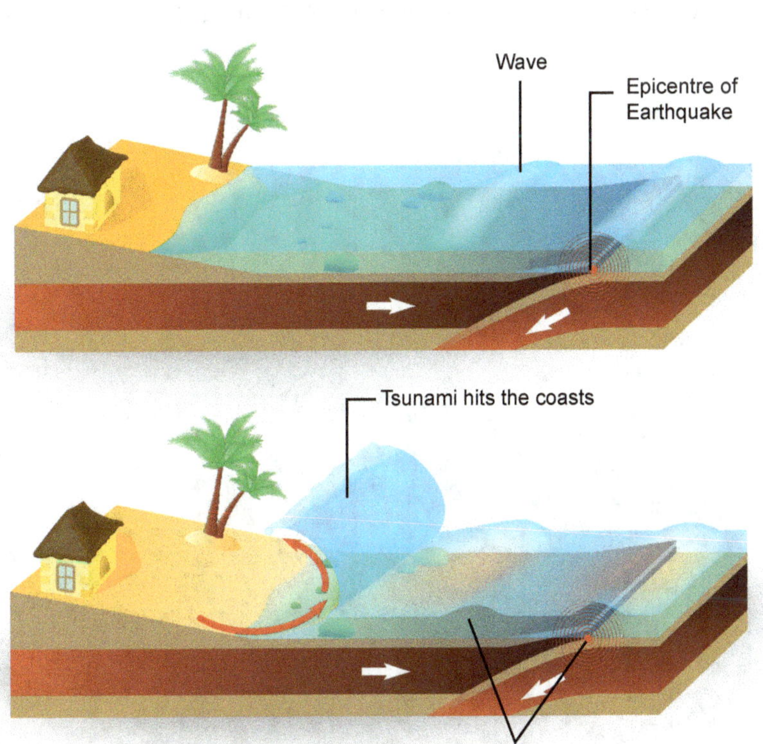

78. Flood

Flood is a condition when overflow of water from a natural water source takes place. For example, overflow of a river in an adjacent plain region during heavy rainfall. When the flood is of high intensity, it causes severe damage. However, at times when the intensity of the flood is low, it can be useful for the plains too, especially for farming. Mild floods leave a layer of fine clay on land which acts as a boon for farming.

The main reasons of flooding are heavy rainfall for a long duration, melting of snow in spring, hurricane and deforestation.

79. Landslide

Landslide is the movement of huge mass of rocks, soil and debris down a slope. This movement is driven by gravitational force or a force that causes two or more parts or layers of the Earth's surface to slide upon in opposite directions. Landslide can occur in two ways:

Rapid landslide: This event takes only a fraction of seconds to occur. It causes huge loss to human life and other natural resources.

Slower landslide: These are slow-paced landslides that may take several hours, days, weeks or even longer to occur.

Some of the main reasons of landslides are gravitational forces, movement of the Earth's plates, prolonged rainfall, inappropriate drainage system, deep excavations on slopes for construction activities, or mining.

80. Drought

Drought is a condition that arises due to lack or insufficiency of rain for a long duration. The main causes of drought are: water shortage, stream flow reduction or depletion of groundwater and soil moisture. It is an indirect but gradual hazard occurring in Nature that affects agriculture.

It can be categorised into four basic kinds:

Permanent: It occurs in dry climatic zones.

Seasonal: It occurs in those climatic zones that experience short annual rainfall and have prolonged dry seasons.

Unpredictable: It can occur due to an abnormal rainfall failure.

Invisible: It occurs when the rate of evaporation is high.

81. Extreme Weather

Extreme weather is a weather condition which is significantly different from the average pattern of weather. Extreme weather is technically an atmospheric disturbance. Some of the examples are: hail and hailstorm, thunder and lightning, hurricane, tornadoes and cyclones. Some other examples are snowstorm and heat waves (loo).

Normal	Extreme
Rain	Hailstorm, thunder, lightning
Wind	Hurricane, tornado, cyclone
Snowfall	Snowstorm
Hot wind	Heat wave/Loo

82. Avalanche

An avalanche is a flow of snow, ice or rock down a mountainside. It is a very sudden event, and can move very fast (about up to 200 km per hour).

There are different kinds of avalanches. Some of them are:

Rock avalanches: They consist of the movement of large segments of shattered rocks.

Ice avalanches: They occur in the vicinity of a glacier, where huge blocks of ice slide.

Debris avalanches: They contain a variety of unconsolidated materials, such as loose stones and soil.

83. Hail and Hailstorm

Hailstorm is an extreme weather condition occurring during rain. Hail forms when rain- drops pass through very cold air in the atmosphere and get frozen into the balls of ice. These balls of ice fall on the ground as hail stones. When the falling of the hail is accompanied by thunderstorm, the resulting condition is known as a hailstorm. Hailstorm develops when the air mass in the atmosphere is unstable and the temperature fall is much greater than the normal.

84. Thunderstorm and Lightning

Thunderstorm develops when tiny particles of ice and water present in the clouds collide with great force. Thunder is an unusual sound occurring during a thunderstorm. This collision causes a series of sudden electrical discharges. These discharges result in sudden flashes of light and trembling sound waves, commonly known as thunder and lightning. Lightning is a bright flash of light that resembles a huge electric spark. Thunderstorm produces hailstorm, rain, high winds and even tornadoes. This extreme weather condition can be fatal to Nature.

A typical thunderstorm is 24 km in diameter and lasts an average of 30 minutes.

85. Hurricanes

A large rotating storm with high wind speed (at least 119 km per hour) in the tropical regions over warm water is called a hurricane or tropical cyclone. Tropical cyclone is the scientific name of hurricane. The main reason behind the occurrence of this cyclone is replacement of warm air mass by a mass of cool air with immense pressure over hot water surface. This movement leads to development of cyclone and formation of a huge storm cloud. If the quantity of warm water is huge then the cycle of storm cloud formation will go on and on and a spinning hurricane will form.

86. Tornadoes

A tornado is a narrow column of high speed air that spins from the cloud towards the ground. It is violent in nature and generally occurs in the spring season. Tornadoes develop before thunderstorm. During a tornado, wind changes its direction at a very high speed. An elevated cone is formed in the atmosphere. The wind blows in a counter-clockwise direction. During tornados the wind speed varies from 177 km to 267 km per hour. Most of the time, the tornado appears transparent till the time it picks up dust and debris or clouds are formed within the funnel.

87. Dust/Sand Storm

Dust storm, also known as sand storm, is a strong and violent form of wind arising mostly during the summer season in dry regions of the Earth. The violent wind carries light-weight, dry and fine particles of clay, dust and other materials to long distances. The minimum speed of wind is about 14 km per hour. The lightest particles flow way above the ground (about 2,000 feet in altitude) and the heavy particles move near the ground. Sometimes, high intensity dust storm affects the local weather and creates unusual sunrise or sunset. Sand storms in Sahara Desert are so intense that they can move a huge sand-dune along.

88. Heat Waves

Heat waves arise when there is an abnormal rise in temperature for a longer duration accompanied with increased level of humidity. These waves are mostly experienced in the months of May-June in the Northern hemisphere. If heat waves continue for a longer duration, they can cause health problems and even death. In the region of low humidity these waves cause crop damage and drought; whereas in the regions of high humidity these waves give rise to health problems, dehydration and even death in severe cases.

89. Landforms

Landform is a geographical feature on the Earth's surface. There are four major and four minor landforms. Major: mountain, hill, plateau and plain. Minor: butte (single hill), canyon (deep, narrow valley with steep sides), valley (depression in the Earth between hills), and basin (a dip or depression in the surface of the land or ocean floor). Formation of landform is a slow process. It takes a long period of time and sometimes millions of years.

Landforms are formed either by movement of tectonic plates or by erosion. Tectonic plates move to form mountains, caves, etc. And erosion by water or wind can create landforms like valleys and canyons.

90. Mountains

Mountains are the highest landforms on the Earth that rise above the surrounding plain area. Their elevation is at least 300 metres or more above the sea level. They are made from huge rocks and stones. The uppermost projected pointed part is known as a peak or summit. Mountains are generally arranged in a line called a range, which consists of a series of peaks and valleys. When arrays of such ranges are linked together, they constitute to form a mountain belt. Younger mountains like the Himalayas of India and the Alps of Europe are generally high and have pointed peaks covered with snow. Mountains are store-houses of valuable natural resources such as: granite, sandstone and marble, which are used as building materials.

Topography: Physical features of land is called topography, for example: mountains, rivers, valleys, etc.

91. Plateaus

Plateaus are high tablelands that have broad and flat tops. These highlands rise sharply above the surrounding area on at least one side. These tablelands are present in every continent. Approximately 40% of total land surface of the Earth is made up of plateaus. The average height of a plateau may range from a few hundred to several thousand metres above the sea level. The shape of this landform can be influenced by erosion. The Tibetan plateau, situated in the North of the Himalayas, is the highest in the world. Most of the plateaus are rich sources of minerals like iron, gold, etc.

92. Plains

Plains are flat surfaces on the Earth that have very gentle slopes. Some plains are formed when rivers deposit the washed-away soil and debris from glaciers, mountains and plateaus. While some are formed when erupting magma flows out and solidifies. Plains cover more than one-third of the world's land area, and exist in every continent. Plains are densely populated as they have fertile soil, abundant water and an ideal climate for human settlements since ancient times. There are three types of plains: floodplain (formed when the flooded river recedes), alluvial plain (formed from steep mountain valley rivers) and coastal plains (lowlands near oceans).

93. Biomes

Biomes are large ecological areas on the Earth, with similar climatic conditions, animals and plant communities. In other words, a biome is a group of several ecosystems present in a particular region. For example, an aquatic biome (water-based biome present in freshwater or sea or ocean) can contain ecosystems such as coral reefs and kelp forests. Biomes are classified in many ways. The simplest and shortest classification has only two biomes: terrestrial (land) and aquatic (water).

Ecosystem: It is a unit where various living organisms live together and depend on one another and the surrounding environment for sustaining life. These living organisms are adapted to the particular environmental conditions in which they live. For example: ponds, one another forests, etc.

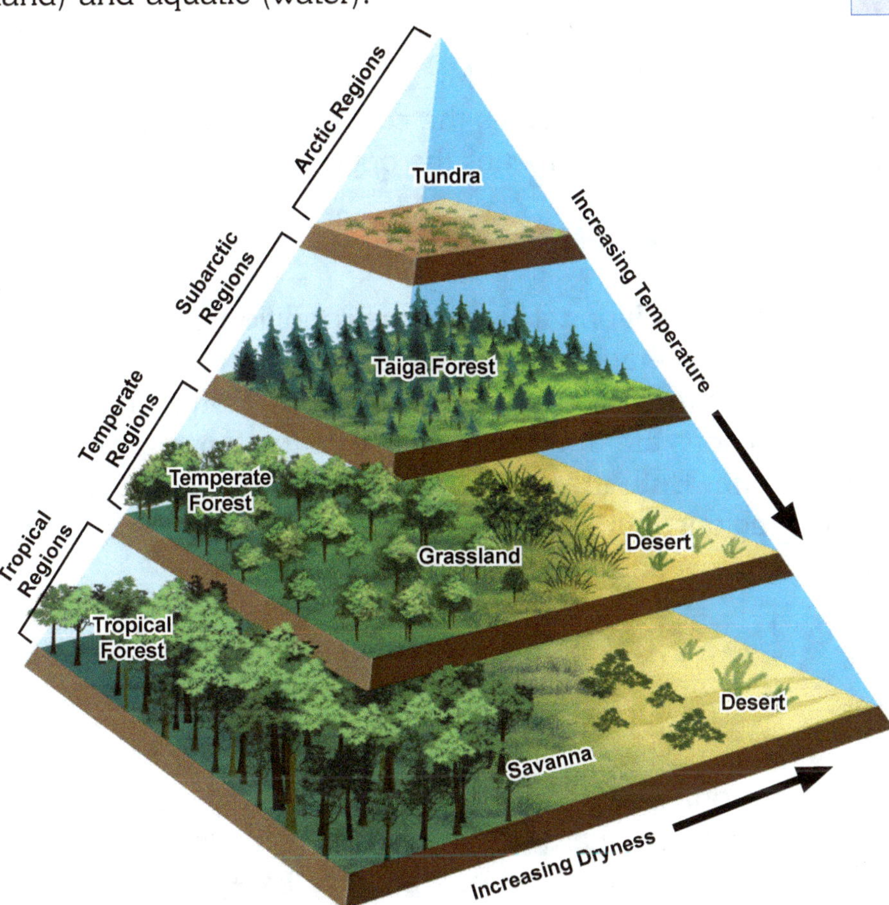

94. Terrestrial or Land Biome

Terrestrial biome means land surface of the Earth where various living organisms live together. These organisms depend on one another as well as on the relative environmental factors. The type of living organisms found in a particular region depends on the physical features of that region such as soil, vegetation and climatic features. Terrestrial biomes are classified on the basis of the similarities between the climatic condition and dominant flora and fauna, e.g. tundra, desert, tropical rainforest, etc.

95. Aquatic Biomes

Aquatic biome is the area of land covered by water that supports life. There are several species of animals and plants that survive in water. They range from the largest animal to the smallest creature of the world.

The aquatic biome can be classified into two basic categories: freshwater and saltwater. Freshwater biome includes those water bodies that contain less than 1% salt in it. For example, lakes, ponds, rivers, streams and wetlands. Saltwater or marine biomes include those water bodies that have salty water. For example, oceans, coral reefs and estuaries.

Arctic

Antarctic

96. Polar Lands

Polar lands are the areas of the Earth that surround the North and the South Pole. These are the frigid zones of the Earth where the temperature remains way below 0°C throughout the year. The polar region surrounding the North Pole is called the Arctic. It includes the Arctic Ocean and northern areas of Europe, Asia and North America. The word 'Arctic' is derived from a Greek word arktos which means 'a bear'. The name signifies the location of a specific constellation, the Ursa Minor above the North Pole. The region surrounding the South Pole is called the Antarctic. It includes the continent of Antarctica and a few parts of the surrounding Southern Ocean. The word 'anti' means the opposite of the Arctic.

97. Extreme Seasons in Polar Lands

Polar lands are known for their extreme weather conditions. This extreme condition is characterised by long, cold winters and short, cool summers. The average temperature ranges from 0° C (summer) to –40° C (winter) in Arctic region and in Antarctic region; it ranges from –28° C (summer) to –60° C (winter). These extreme low temperature conditions are due to the, shape of the Earth, position of the poles and the tilt of the Earth towards the Sun. Both the poles never get direct sunlight and the Sun is always low on the horizon. In the polar regions, during the summer season the Sun never sets whereas during the winter season the sun never rises and there is complete darkness.

98. Land Around a Frozen Ocean

The Arctic is referred as the land around the frozen ocean. The region consists of the Arctic Ocean and the surrounding land, including Greenland and Spitsbergen, and the northern parts of Alaska, Canada, Norway and Russia. Some of the land parts of the Arctic are covered with ice caps, such as Greenland. Others have rich tundra which is not glaciated. Most of the Arctic is uninhabitable with no fertility in terms of agriculture. This region is sparsely populated. The Arctic has some important mineral resources such as coal, oil, nickel, iron and tin.

99. Plants and Animals of Arctic Lands

The Arctic has no trees but the ground is covered with grasses, mosses and dry-looking plants. These plants do not flower and are adapted to the tundra climate. The animals found on the Arctic are distinct from the animals found in the Antarctic region, as the Arctic is warmer than the Antarctic. Some of the Arctic animals are polar bear, arctic fox, snowy owl, arctic reindeer, musk ox, etc. These animals have some specific features, e.g. small legs and ears, blubber layer under the skin for insulation, covering of hair etc. These specific features support them to live in such extreme conditions.

100. Antarctic Water

Antarctica, the coldest, driest and windiest continent, is an ice-covered region with several small associated islands. This continent is mostly glaciated. The tiny ice crystals that form in the Antarctic region are purely water. There is no salt in it. So, the frozen glaciers and icebergs are pure water. This means the more the ice crystals are formed, the more the salt is left behind in the ocean water. The high concentration of salt in the water makes the water heavy. Heavier liquids freeze at lower temperatures than lighter liquids and remain in a frozen state for a long time. This makes the Antarctic region extremely cold.

101. Antarctic Plants and Animals

The climate of the Antarctic is so harsh that it is not suitable for dense vegetation. Plants found in this region are non-woody and simple like algae, mosses, liverworts, lichens and microscopic fungi. There are a few types of insects such as mites and spring tails that feed on the Antarctic plants. The animals have specific physical features to fight the chill and reduce the loss of body heat for survival:

- Thick, windproof or waterproof coats
- Thick fat (or blubber) layers beneath the skin
- Small extremities to conserve heat loss

102. Adelei Penguins and Birds

Adelei Penguins, the sliding and diving birds, are the main inhabitants of the Antarctic. They cannot run or walk very fast, but they slide well on smooth ice surface on their bellies and can travel a long distance like this. Their wings are in form of flippers that help them to swim in the icy water. They swim at a speed of 40 kmph while catching prey or escaping from a predator. They build nests on small stone-shaped rocks.

Birds near the Antarctic can be seen during the spring time. More than 100 kinds of birds visit the Antarctic coastline and offshore islands. Most of the birds fly over the ocean towards the Antarctic to build their nests over the wide open area. A few species of the birds found in the Antarctic region are albatrosses, petrels, skuas, gulls and terns.

ARCTIC OCEAN
Queen Elizabeth Is.
LINCOLN SEA
GREENLAND (DENMARK)
Prince Patrick I.
Axel Heiberg
ELLESMERE I.
Cape York
Cape Brew
Qeqertarsuaq
NUUK
REYKJAVIK
ICELAND
Nunap Isua
EAST SIBERIAN SEA
CHUKCHI SEA
Point Barrow
Cape Hope
RUSSIA
ALASKA (USA)
BEAUFORT SEA
BANKS ISLAND
VICTORIA ISLAND
Amundsen Gulf
Mc Clure Strait
Melville I.
Parry Channel
Prince of Wales I.
Bathurst I.
Cornwallis I.
Somerset I.
Devon I.
Bylot I.
BAFFIN BAY
Baffin Bay
Prince Charles I.
Southampton I.
King William I.
Foxe Basin
Mansel I.
Coats I.
Denmark Strait
Grimsey
Rifa
Arctic Circle
BERING SEA
St. Lawrence I.
St. Matthew I.
Nunivak I.
Pribilof Is
Kodiak I.
Gulf of Alaska
L. Great Bear
L. Great Slave
L. Athabasca
Peace
Nelson
Cape Churchill
HUDSON BAY
JAMES BAY
La Grande Rivière
Belcher Is.
LABRADOR SEA
Cape Chidley
DUBLIN
IRELAND
Eng
ALEUTIAN ISLANDS
Queen Charlotte I.
Vancouver I.
CANADA
L. Winnipeg
L. Reindeer
Albany
L. Superior
L. Huron
L. Michigan
L. Ontario
L. Erie
St. Lawrence
Prince Edward I.
Cape Breton I.
Sable I.
ST JOHN'S
Miquelon
OTTAWA
NORTH PACIFIC OCEAN
Cape Mendocino
Point Conception
Channel Is.
Pt. Eugenia
UNITED STATES OF AMERICA
WASHINGTON, D.C.
Missouri
Mississippi
Rio Grande
Brazos
Snake
Gulf of California
Long I.
Cape May
Cape Cod
MASSACHUSETTS BAY
CHESAPEAKE BAY
Cape Hatteras
HAMILTON
BERMUDA
NORTH ATLANTIC OCEAN
Cape Fister
PORTUGAL
LISBON
Azores
PONTA DELGADA
FUNCHAL
GIBRALTAR
Hawaiian Islands
Tropic of Cancer
Nihoa Kauai
Moloka Lāna
Hawai
Johnston I.
MEXICO
Cape San Lucas
Gulf of Mexico
Gulf of Campeche
BAHAMAS
NASSAU
BAHAMA IS.
SARGASSO SEA
Canary Is
Cabo Bojador
W. SAHARA
MAURIT
NOU
DAKAR
SENEG
Cape Verde Is
CAPE VERDE
PRAIA
MEXICO CITY
Jamaica
Puerto Rico (USA)
Lesser Antilles
ATLANTIC OCEAN
INDEX
COUNTRY   CAPITAL
1 GUATEMALA   GUATEMALA CITY
2 EL SALVADOR   SAN SALVADOR
3 HONDURAS   TEGUCIGALPA
4 NICARAGUA   MANAGUA
5 COSTA RICA   SAN JOSE
6 PANAMA   PANAMA CITY
7 BELIZE   BELMOPAN
8 CUBA   HAVANA
9 JAMAICA   KINGSTON
10 HAITI   PORT-AU-PRINCE
11 DOMINICAN REP. SANTO DOMINGO
Palmyra Atoll
Tabuaeran
Kiritimati
KIRIBATI
Baker I.
Equator
Galapagos Is
Isabela
Santa Cruz
Punta Galera
Punta Negra
CARACAS
VENEZUELA
GEORGETOWN
PARAMARIBO
CAYENNE
FRENCH GUIANA
GUYANA
SURINAME
COLOMBIA
BOGOTA
QUITO
ECUADOR
Ponta de Jericoacoara
Cape Pal
PHOENIX IS
Starbuck
Malden
Vostok
Penrhyn
COOK ISLANDS
Manihiki
Marquesas I.
PERU
LIMA
BRAZIL
BRASILIA
Cape de Sao Roque
Asce
PINE ISLANDS POLYNESIA
FRENCH POLYNESIA (FR.)
SOUTH PACIFIC OCEAN
SAMOA
APIA
AMERICAN SAMOA
PAGO PAGO
NIUE
PAPEETE
Bora Bora
Tatakoto
Tubuai
Tematagi
Tuamotu
BOLIVIA
LA PAZ
SUCRE
Ponta da Baleia
Is. Martin Vaz
NUKUALOFA
TONGA
COOK IS.
Rarotonga
Mangaia
PARAGUAY
ASUNCION
Cape de Sao Tome
Cape Frio
Tropic of Capricorn
Kermadec Islands
SANTIAGO
URUGUAY
MONTEVIDEO
BUENOS AIRES
Cape San Antonio
Cape Corrientes
Cape de Santa Marta Grande
SO
ATL
OC
Chatham Islands
International Date Line
CHILE
Juan Fernandez Is
Punta Lavapie
Chiloe I.
ARGENTINA
Cape Dos Bahias
Cape Tres Puntas
STANLEY
FALKLAND IS.
Cape de Hornos
Cape San Diego
Staten I.
SCOTIA SEA
Antarctic Circle
Elephant I.
Livingston I.
Anvers I.
Biscoe Is.
South Shetland Is.
Joinville I.
James Ross I.
Cape Framnes
Peter I I.
Charcot I.
Cape Jeremi
Cape Agassiz
ROSS SEA
AMUNDSEN SEA
Siple I.
Burke I.
Thurston I.
Farwell I.
BELLINGSHAUSEN SEA
MARGUERITE BAY
Alexander I.
Lady I.
Spaatz I.
WEDDELL SEA
Cape Norvegia
Lyddan I.
Orthomorphic Projection

THE WEST INDIES (Lesser Antilles)
Puerto Rico (US)
Virgin Is. (UK)
ROAD TOWN
ANGUILLA (UK)
CHARLOTTE AMALIE
Virgin Is. (US)
Neth. Antilles (Neth. Ant.)
ANTIGUA & BARBUDA
BASSETERRE
ST. JOHN'S
SAINT CHRISTOPHER NEVIS
MONTSERRAT (U.K.)
PLYMOUTH
GUADELOUPE (FR.)
BASSE-TERRE
DOMINICA
ROSEAU
MARTINIQUE (FR.)
FORT-DE-FRANCE
CASTRIES
ST. LUCIA
Leeward Islands
Lesser Antilles
Windward Islands
ATLANTIC OCEAN
CARIBBEAN SEA
KINGSTOWN
ST. VINCENT & THE GRENADINES
BARBADOS
BRIDGE TOWN
ST. GEORGE'S
GRENADA
TRINIDAD & TOBAGO
TOBAGO
PORT OF SPAIN
VENEZUELA
SOUTH AMERICA

INDEX		
	COUNTRY	CAPITAL
12	GAMBIA	BANJUL
13	GUINEA BISSAU	BISSAU
14	GUINEA	CONAKRY
15	SIERRA LEONE	FREETOWN
16	LIBERIA	MONROVIA
17	COAST D'IVOIRE	YAMOUSSOUKRO
18	GHANA	ACCRA
19	TOGO	LOME
20	BENIN	PORTO-NOVO
21	BURKINA FASO	OUAGADOUGOU
22	EQ. GUINEA	MALABO
23	RWANDA	KIGALI
24	BURUNDI	BUJUMBURA
25	KUWAIT	KUWAIT
26	BAHRAIN	MANAMA
27	QATAR	DOHA
28	CYPRUS	LEFKOSIA
29	LEBANON	BEIRUT
30	JORDAN	AMMAN
31	ISRAEL	JERUSALEM
32	GEORGIA	TBILISI
33	ARMENIA	YEREVAN
34	AZERBAIJAN	BAKU
35	ESTONIA	TALLINN
36	LATVIA	RIGA
37	NETHERLANDS	THE HAGUE
38	BELGIUM	BRUSSELS
39	CZECH REPUBLIC	PRAGUE
40	SLOVAKIA	BRATISLAVA
41	AUSTRIA	VIENNA
42	HUNGARY	BUDAPEST
43	SWITZERLAND	BERN
44	SLOVENIA	LJUBLJANA
45	CROATIA	ZAGREB
46	SAN MARINO	SAN MARINO
47	SERBIA	BELGRADE
48	BOSNIA AND HERZ.	SARAJEVO
49	MONTENEGRO	PODGORICA
50	KOSOVO	PRISTINA
51	BULGARIA	SOFIA
52	MACEDONIA	SKOPJE
53	ALBANIA	TIRANA
54	VATICAN CITY	VATICAN CITY
55	MOLDOVA	CHISINAU
56	LIECHTENSTEIN	VADUZ

Mountain

Hill

103. Mountains and Hills

Mountains and hills are the elevated landforms. There are several similarities and dissimilarities between mountains and hills:

- Unlike mountains, hills are less steep and do not have very high elevations. However, both mountain and hill have a definite peak each, which is its highest point.
- Mountains are usually connected with other mountains and adjacent hills, whereas hills may mount individually, too.
- Mountains are mostly rocky, whereas hills can be made up of soil, mud and the combination of rocks and soil.
- Elevation range of Hills: ≤ 300 metres above the sea level.
- Elevation range of mountains: ≥ 300 metres above the sea level.

104. Formation of Mountains

A mountain formation starts when two tectonic plates collide. The colliding plates either subduct or uplift. Subduction means sliding of the oceanic crust below the continental crust. And uplift means upward movement of crust due to the movements of tectonic plates. Mountain formation started several million years ago when the continents were forming. During that time several collisions between the plates took place and several mountain ranges formed in every continent. Some of the significant formations are:

- Formation of the Himalayas: The Himalayas were formed by the collision of the Indo-Australian plate and the Eurasian plate.

- Formation of the Cascade mountain range: The Cascade mountain

Subduct

Uplift

range (Mount St. Helens) is formed by the subduction of the oceanic crust of the Juan de Fuca plate below the continental crust of the North American plate.

105. Fold Mountains

Fold Mountains are the most common type of mountains in the world. They are formed where two or more Earth's tectonic plates are pushed together. At the region where the collision takes place, the boundaries of the plates are compressed together moving the rocks and debris outwards giving rise to outcropped landform on the surface of the Earth–the mountain. These mountains are rocky and their formation is often associated with continental crust. The process by which these mountains are formed is called Orogency. Orogenic events are very slow and take millions of years. The Appalachian Mountain of the valley-and-ridge region of eastern United States, and the Alps of Europe are some of the major examples of Fold Mountains.

106. Dome Mountains

Dome Mountains are formed when a hot layer of molten magma pushes up the surface of the Earth but doesn't crack through it. Slowly, the magma cools down and hardens into rocks. These mountains are not so high as folded mountains. Domes are flat, dissected surfaces which are sloping gradually towards the surrounding basins. The diameter of the base of a Dome Mountain ranges up to hundreds of kilometres. The Black Hills of South Dakota are the examples of larger domes and the Henry Mountains of Utah are the examples of small domes.

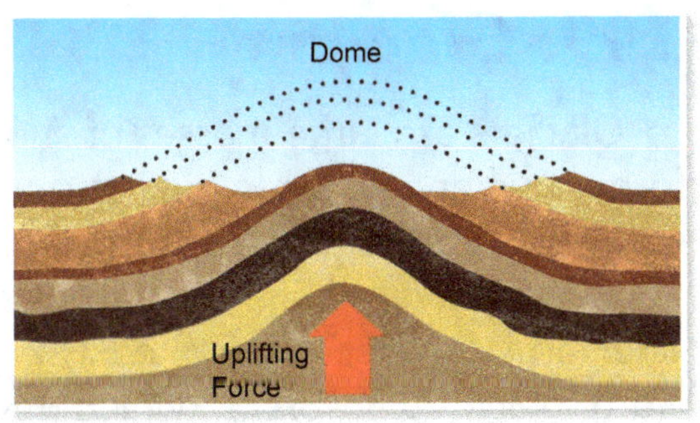

107. Fault-block Mountains

Faults refer to the cracks on the Earth's crust. Sometimes some internal forces of the underground earth inflict a huge pressure on the Earth's crust. This pressure pulls apart some part of the Earth's crust. Due to which some parts of the Earth are pushed upward and the adjoining parts collapse.

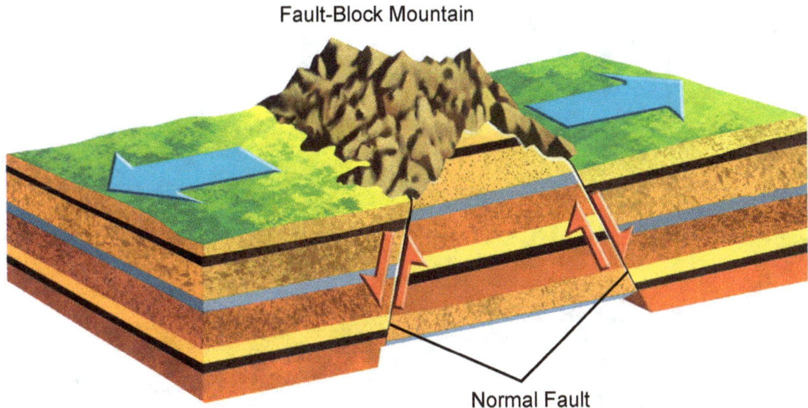

These movements move the rocky layer of the earth and are accompanied by earthquakes. The formation of these types of mountain's takes a long period of time and an intense internal pressure. In the Great Basin in Nevada, hundreds of such blocks of rocks have risen above the dry surrounding plains. The Sierra Nevada range of California is also a good example of fault-block mountains.

108. Volcanic Mountains

Volcanic mountains are made up of lava, ash and cinders, which pour out from within the Earth and gather at the surface. When the ash and lava cools, it forms a cone-shaped mountain. The usual volcano rock has a large hole or crater at the top of it.

Some of the most famous volcanic mountains or peaks are:

North America: Mount Rainier in Washington, Mount Shasta

California: Mount Katmai in Alaska, and Mount Mauna Loa in Hawaii

South America: Mount Misti and Aconcagua

Asia: Mount Fujiyama in Japan

Europe: Mount Vesuvius in Italy

Cinder: It is a rock that is formed when magma reaches the Earth's surface and cools quickly. It is similar to pumice, which has several cavities and low density. Cinder can float on water.

Crater: It is a bowl-shaped geological formation at the top of a volcano.

109. Glaciers

Glaciers are large masses of snow. These are formed when snow remains at one location for a very long time and turns into ice. They have ability to move, hence are called 'rivers of ice'. The term 'glacier' originated from the French word glace (glah-SAY), which means ice. At present, they occupy about 10% of the world's land. Most of them are located in the polar regions. Some of the glaciers move only a few centimetres a day while some can move about 50 metres a day. The fast-moving glaciers are called galloping glaciers.

Alpine Glaciers

110. Types of Glaciers

Glaciers are categorised into two groups: alpine glaciers and ice sheets. Alpine glaciers (valley glaciers or mountain glaciers) originate from the mountainsides and move downward towards valleys. The Gorner Glacier in Switzerland and the Furtwangler Glacier in Tanzania are some of the examples of alpine glaciers. Ice sheet glaciers have broad domes and spread out from centre in all directions. Their domes are so wide that they cover everything around valleys, plains and even oceans. The largest ice sheet, called the continental glacier, spreads over vast areas. Today, continental glaciers cover most of the Antarctica and the island of Greenland.

Ice Sheets

111. Valley

A valley is a relatively flat, low land lying between ranges of hills and mountains on the Earth's surface. Valleys are generally formed by erosion caused by rivers or glaciers. They can be classified on the basis of shape or origin. On the basis of shape, they can be categorised as: V-shape and U-shape. And on the basis of origin, valleys can be classified as river valleys and glacial valleys. River valleys are generally V-shaped valleys and are formed by flowing water of the river. Glacial valleys are mostly U-shaped valleys that are formed by glacial melting and erosion.

V-Shaped Valley

U-Shaped Valley

112. Types of Plains

Plains are one of the most widespread landforms of the Earth. They are primarily classified on the basis of the process of formation. The three main types of plains are: structural plains, depositional plains and erosional plains.

Types of plains	Description	
1. Structural Plains	Structural plains make the most extensive lowlands on the Earth's surface. They are mainly formed by the uplift of continental shelf or seafloor. Examples are: the South Eastern Plains and the Great Plains province of the USA, etc.	
2. Depositional Plains	Depositional plains are created by deposition of materials brought by natural agents of transport like wind, rivers, glaciers and waves. Examples are: Nile Delta area of Egypt, Gangetic Plains of India, etc.	
3. Erosional Plains	Erosional plains are also known as pene plains. They are formed by the various natural erosion agents such as running water, rivers, wind and glaciers. Examples are: Canadian Shield, West Siberian plains, etc.	

Erosion is a natural process that creates or destroys the landforms of the Earth. The common erosion agents are: wind and water. The landforms created by erosion are: flood plains and sandbars. This is called fluvial erosion in which deposition and accumulation of debris takes place. In case of destructive erosion, wind or water wears down large rocks or mountains. The landforms formed by this process are valleys and canyons.

113. Grasslands

Grasslands are the open and flat plains on the Earth where grass is the most dominating flora. The grasslands present in the Southern hemisphere get more rainfall than those in the Northern hemisphere. Hence the grass in the Southern hemisphere grows more than 2 metres in height and its roots extend several feet into the soil.

Grasslands are categorised into two types on the basis of climatic conditions of the Earth.

Tropical grasslands: These grass-covered areas are warm throughout the year but at the same time receive moderate to heavy rainfall.

Temperate grasslands: These grass-covered areas receive only 25 to 75 centimetres of rain per year.

114. Savanna

Savanna is a type of flat grassland in tropical and subtropical regions, bordering tropical rainforests. However, certain dry savannas are present on the borders of some deserts as well. These grasslands are generally warm and they have dry climatic conditions. They are characterised by brushy and coarse grasses with a few small or dispersed trees

that form a scattered sunshade. These scattered sunshades help sunlight to reach the land directly. Since these grasslands are close to rainforests, they witness long rainy seasons. However, as the distance increases, the savannas become dry and hot. One of the largest savannas on the Earth is the African savanna. Other major savannas are found in South America, Australia, India, the Myanmar (Burma)–Thailand region in Asia and Madagascar.

Tree Canopy: The layer of overlapping leaves, branches and stems of the tall trees that provides shade to the smaller plants underneath.

115. Steppe

A steppe is a dry and grassy belt of grassland. It is located in temperate climatic regions of the Earth, which lie between the tropics and the polar regions. They are also called mid-latitude grasslands. The two main types of grasses which are found in this area are cropland and pasture. These are short grasses, which are mostly used for grazing by sheep, goats, horses, camels and cattle.

Steppes receive about 25-50 centimetres of rainfall (enough for only short grass growth) every year. The largest temperate grassland in the world is the Eurasian steppe (it extends from Hungary to China). Other example of steppes is the dry, short grass prairie of North America's Great Plains.

116. Canyons

Canyons are deep V-shaped narrow valleys with steep sides and rocky boundaries. The word 'Canyon' is derived from the Spanish word cañon, which means tube or pipe. These are formed by the movement of rivers (river canyons), the process of weathering and erosion (weathering canyons), and tectonic activities underneath the Earth's surface (submarine canyon).

Canyon-Type	Example
River Canyon	Hells Canyon on Snake river
Weathering Canyon	Canyonlands National Park, Utah
Submarine Canyon	Zemchung Canyon in the Bering Sea

117. Caves

Caves are the underground enclosure with access from the surface of the ground or from the sea. They are the natural openings of the Earth. Caves are formed by two methods:

- Weathering of rocks; or
- Through water seepage under the ground: Water flows through the cracks present on the Earth's surface, dissolving certain underground rocks made up of limestone which creates deep hollow shafts.

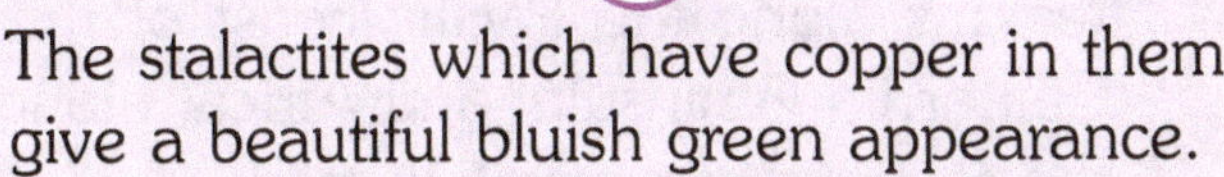

The world's longest cave is Mammoth Cave in Kentucky, USA.

118. Stalactites and Stalagmites

Stalactites and Stalagmites are natural features present in caves. These are deposits of minerals which form on cave roof, cave floor or near cave walls. Stalactites hang from the ceilings of caves like icicles, while stalagmites resemble traffic cones that look like emerging from the ground. These features form when water droplets containing some amount of lime and other minerals drip down from the cracks on the cave ceiling. While dripping down some part of water gets evaporated, leaving behind lime deposits. These lime deposits gather to form hanging structures called stalactites. When the dripping water reaches cave floor, it gives rise to thick columns called stalagmites which are of short height.

The stalactites which have copper in them give a beautiful bluish green appearance.

Icicle: It is a formation of ice which resembles a pendent spear. It is formed when the water dripping from an object freezes.

119. Hot Desert

Hot desert is any location on the Earth that is extremely dry and receives less than 25 cm of rainfall per year. Deserts may be very hot or very cold. In hot deserts, the Sun shines mercilessly and the only source of water is through meagre annual rainfall. African and Asian deserts are the examples of hot deserts. African desert is hot since it is close to the equator and Asian desert is hot because it is far away from the sea. Cacti are one of the main plants found in the hot desert. Hot deserts are further classified into two classes: sand deserts and rock deserts. Sand deserts have abundant sand and wind creates huge sand-dunes in this region; whereas rock deserts have bare rocks, rough plains and cliffs.

Sand-Dune: It is a mound created by the accumulation of sand grains. It is built by wind and can even get displaced by it.

120. Cold Desert

Cold deserts are those deserts where main source of water is snow. They are also called temperate deserts. These are located at a higher altitude and have dry environment. The dry atmosphere is due to the presence of high mountains between the coastal region and the desert zone. The Gobi desert in Mongolia is a classic example of a cold plateau desert. The temperature difference between summer (32°C) and winter (–4°C) in Gobi desert is significant. This desert has very few sand-dunes and is mostly flat plain with a thin stony covering.

121. Mild Desert

Mild deserts are generally found near the tropical regions along the west coasts of continents. These are high-altitude areas where the annual rainfall is less than 250 mm but the temperature is significantly lower than that of hot deserts. The weather of the mild desert is influenced by cooler but dry winds. These types of deserts are located in the following areas: South America, the Atacama Desert near to the Pacific Ocean; regions along the Pacific coast of the Baja California Peninsula; and Africa, along with the sections of coastal Namibia.

122. The Great Desert: Sahara

The Sahara, the great African desert, is located in the Northern part of Africa. On the eastern side of the Sahara, the Red Sea and on the western part, the Atlantic Ocean is located. The northern part of the Sahara Desert is adjoining the Mediterranean Sea, while in the south the ancient, immobile sand-dunes are located. It is the largest hot desert in the world. It covers about 10 per cent of the continent (spreads over 5632704 km^2). Yearly rainfall here is not more than 25 cm. The day temperature reaches around 50° C and the night temperature falls to less than 0° C. Sand sheets and sand-dunes cover approximately 25 per cent of the Sahara's surface. The major water source of the Sahara is the seasonal stream. The Nile is the only permanent river that flows from Central Africa to the Mediterranean Sea.

The name Sahara is derived from the Arabic noun Sahra, meaning desert.

The Rann of Kutch located in Gujarat, India, is a white desert plain mainly composed of salt. It Is the largest seasonal wetland where water gathered in the monsoon evaporates and leaves behind a white desert plain during the winter season.

123. Indian Desert: Thar

The Thar Desert is also known as the Great Indian Desert. The name 'Thar' is taken from a regional term Thal, which means dry. Some parts of this desert are located in the state of Rajasthan, north-western India and some in Punjab and Sind region of eastern Pakistan. This desert spreads over 200,000 km^2 area. From the west, the Thar is irrigated by the Indus River plain, and in the southeast it is surrounded by the Aravalli Range. The wetland 'Rann of Kutch' is located on the south of the Thar. The monsoon winds which are the source of rain for the Indian subcontinent, generally bypass the Thar region and hence the annual rainfall remains less than 10 cm in west and 50 cm in east.

125. Temperate Forest

Temperate forests are the regions experiencing high level of rainfall, humidity and snowfall (between 20-60 inches per year). They are located approximately 25° and 50° latitude in both hemispheres.

These forests are known for their wide range of temperatures [from hot in summer (about 30°C) to extremely cold in winter (about –30°C)]. This climatic feature makes them different from other types of forests. Temperate forests have thick soil humus, which supports a wide range of plant life and wild life. A variety of deciduous trees are found in this region. Animals of temperate forests are adapted to the cold and lack of food in winter. These forests are located in Eastern Asia, part of Russia, Central and Western Europe and Eastern United States.

Coniferous Trees: These trees have needles instead of broad leaves, and their seeds grow inside protective, woody cones.

124. Tropical Rainforest

The Tropical rainforest is a region experiencing constant temperature and heavy rainfall. The climate is mostly hot and humid with daily rainfall and wet surroundings. These forests are covered with lush green trees and plants, which grow very close and form a canopy. Annual rainfall is around 50 to 260 inches. Around 6% of the Earth's surface is covered with rainforests. Hence, it is estimated that almost 40% of the Earth's oxygen is produced by the rainforest trees. The largest rainforests are located in Brazil (South America), Zaire (Africa) and Indonesia (South-East Asia). Some other prominent tropical rainforests are located in Hawaii and the islands of the Pacific and Caribbean region.

Deciduous Trees: The trees which change their leaf colour in autumn and shed leaves in winter.

126. Taiga Forest

Taiga (boreal) forests, also called the coniferous forests, are located in the north of the mid-latitude forest land. These are thick forests having trees such as spruce, pine, fir, etc. They cover about 9% of the world's land. These forests have long cold winters and short summers.

The world's largest taiga is located in Russia. It spreads in an area of about 5,800 km² from the Pacific Ocean to the Ural Mountains. Other places which have taiga forests are: Alaska, Canada, Scandinavia and Siberia. Birds native to the taiga usually migrate south during the freezing winter months.

127. Amazing Amazon

Amazon rainforest is the world's largest tropical rainforest. It covers around 6,000,000 km² area of Brazil, which is about 40% of Brazil's total area. It occupies the drainage basin of the Amazon River (second largest river in the world) and its tributaries in northern South America. This region experiences high rainfall, high humidity and constant high temperature. It is famous for its immense biodiversity. Flora and fauna in the region is so immense that only 10% of it is known to zoologists. Piranha, sting ray, manatee, water snake and anaconda (giant snake that has a length of about 30 feet), monkey, jaguar and a vast insect and bird population are the major species found in the Amazon.

One of the largest freshwater fish found in the Amazon is the Pirarucu (also known as the arapaima or paiche). A menacing meat-eater, the pirarucu guzzles up other fish and can grow to nearly 3m long. Tapir is the largest forest animal found in the Amazon.

128. Magical Madagascar

Madagascar is the fourth largest island in the world, after Greenland, New Guinea and Borneo. It is located about 400 km off the south-eastern coast of Africa in the Indian Ocean. Madagascar as an island is a combination of plateaus, coastal plains and beaches. The tropical rainforests of Madagascar lie in the low-elevation, due to which sometimes it is also called the 'lowland rainforest'. This rainforest has dense tree canopies in it. The average rainfall is recorded about 200 cm annually in the north-western region. Madagascar has about 250,000 species of animals and 12,000 species of plants. Ring-tailed lemurs, African sunset moths, coloured lizards, etc. are some of them. One of the most famous plants is the baobab tree.

129. Cloud Forest

The Monteverde cloud forest of Costa Rica is also known as the fog forest. These are tropical or subtropical evergreen forests. They are popular for 100% humidity and heavy rainfall, which is due to the surrounding clouds and mist. This forest contains short and crooked trees, trunks of which are usually covered with a thick layer of mosses, climbing ferns, lichens and air plants (such as orchids). Certain plants like begonias, ferns and a few varieties of herbaceous plants attain a large size in the flat clear zones of the forest. The trees in this forest are called elfin as they are short in height.

130. Peculiar Plants of Rainforest

Rainforests are the region of dense plantation and have a huge variety of flora and fauna. Some of the peculiar plants that possess striking features are given below.

Giant titan arum (Indonesian rainforest):
It is the most stinking plant that produces a peculiar smell of a decomposing mammal to attract insects.

Durian fruit:
Durian fruit has an amazing smell that can be detected about one kilometre away.

Rafflesia (Borneo Rainforest):
It is the biggest flower on the Earth. It is a parasitic plant that has foul smell to attract insects.

131. Indian Forests

India is famous for its diverse wildlife, and dense and vast forest-cover. Forests cover the second largest land-share after agriculture, which is about 6,780,000 km² (about 20.64% of the total land of the country). More than 45,000 plant species and more than 80,000 animal species thrive in the Indian forests.

The several types of forests in India are:

Kerala	Rainforests
Ladakh	Alpine pastures
Rajasthan	Arid desert vegetation
Northeast	Evergreen forests
Western Ghats	Wet evergreen
Eastern Himalayas	Semi-evergreen
Madhya Pradesh	Dry deciduous (the Satpura range)
Shivalik Hills	Dry evergreen

132. Fresh Water

Water on the Earth's surface is categorised into two categories: salty water and fresh water. Fresh water is the water that contains less than 1000 milligrams per litre of dissolved solids (most often salt). Natural glaciers and icebergs, ice sheets and ice caps, bogs, ponds, lakes, rivers and streams, and groundwater in aquifers and underground streams are some of the examples of fresh water. Fresh water is the only form of water which is potable, leaving some exceptions which need proper purification before making it fit for drinking.

133. Rivers

Any natural stream of water that flows through a channel is called a river. A river has a defined bank bedded with sand and gravel. The water in a river comes from different sources, such as rain water, melting snow and ice, and from springs and some part from lakes. Rivers carry rain and other forms of the Earth's surface water to the sea, or to other rivers that enter dry plains and inland lakes. This is a continuous way to regulate the Earth's water cycle. Large rivers have many tributaries or smaller streams that flow into the main stream.

Tributary: A river or stream that flows into a larger river or lake is called a tributary.

134. River Basin

A land that is drained by a river and its tributaries is called the river basin. A basin sends all the water collected in it to a central river which is connected to the ocean. Basins are generally divided into two parts: watersheds and areas around a smaller river, lake or stream. Many smaller watersheds make a big river basin. River basins support life and agriculture of a particular region. River basin plains are very fertile as they get deposits of mineral from the adjoining flowing river. For example, the Gangetic River Basin in India is densely populated and dependent on River Ganga, especially for agriculture.

Watershed: It is a land piece that is drained by a river system.

135. Lakes

Lake Baikal in Russia is the deepest lake in the world that holds about 20% of the Earth's unfrozen surface water.

Any large water-body that is surrounded by land is called a lake. Lakes are generally defined as temporary water-bodies and are one of the most valuable and beautiful natural resources on the Earth. Lakes are found in every environment (mountains, deserts, plains or near seashores) and in all the continents. These vary greatly in length and depth as well. Small lakes are called ponds and very big lakes are called seas. The water in lakes comes from rain, melting ice, snow and ground water seepage. Most of the lakes contain fresh water. Lakes are classified into three ways: (1) on the basis of the types of nutrients the lakes have, (2) on the basis of the way water mixes, and (3) on the basis of the kinds of fish that live in them.

The continents such as North America, Africa and Asia contain about 70% of the total lake water of the world.

136. Springs and Fountains

A spring is water stream flowing out from a natural opening or a crack in the ground. Springs can be found in the bottom of a valley or near the sides of hills or near any form of rock. They are classified into three categories: seepage, artesian and tubular springs. Seepage springs are small water puddles formed when ground water seeps out on the surface. Artesian springs are formed when ground water seeps through faults in the ground and flows in valleys. Tubular springs are large springs associated with caves. Fountains are streams of water that shoots out from ground into the air. The source of fountains is a natural spring.

Spring

Fountain

137. Waterfall

Waterfall is a natural water-body. Water stream takes a sudden and steep drop in it, for example, at the edge of a cliff. Waterfall usually forms a pool at the bottom. And if the water in the pool overflows, it continues as a river or another waterfall. They are found in those regions where cliffs, cracks or faults are present along with huge rocks. There are two types of waterfalls: cataract and cascade. A huge waterfall is called a cataract and when a water stream falls over a slanting rock, it is called a cascade. The tallest waterfall of the world is the Angel Falls, located in Venezuela.

Waterfall

138. The Nile

The Nile is the world's longest river. Its name is derived from a Greek word Neilos, which means valley. It has a length of about 6,650 km and it lies in Africa, and flows through countries such as: Kenya, Eritrea, Congo, Burundi, Uganda, Tanzania, Rwanda, Egypt, Sudan and Ethiopia. This river has deep rooted links with Ancient Egypt's history. These links are reflected in the locations of the historical sites of Egypt, which are located along the banks of the Nile river, for example, Luxor and Cairo cities. It provides a fertile green valley across the desert in Egypt. Lake Victoria and Lake Tana are the major lakes associated with it. It drains into the Mediterranean Sea at the Nile Delta in Northern Egypt.

139. Sea

A sea is a huge water-body with salty water. Geographically, it is defined as a division of an ocean, which is partially surrounded by land. Seas play a key role in defining the Earth's climate since they are a major part of the water cycle. The temperature of the sea mainly depends on the amount of solar radiation it absorbs. The sea is a natural habitat of several plants and animals. The major seas of the world include Mediterranean Sea, Caribbean Sea and South China Sea.

140. Sea Level

The place where the sea and air meet is called the sea level. Sea level is used as the base level to measure all the elevation and depth on the Earth. There is a great variation in the sea level at every locality due to the changes in tides, atmospheric pressure and wind conditions. Other than these factors, the Earth's changing climates and global warming also influence the sea level. Mean sea level can be calculated by averaging the heights of these levels at all stages of the tides (low and high) over a long period of time.

141. South China Sea

The South China Sea is a segment of the Pacific Ocean. The average depth of this sea is 5,419 feet. It is located between eastern Vietnam, western Philippines (Southeast Asia), northern Indonesia, Singapore, northeastern Malay peninsula (Malaysia), South of mainland China, and the island of Taiwan. The Pearl, Min, Jiulong and the Red are the major rivers which flow into it. The South China Sea is rich in marine life. Large reserves of oil and natural gas have been discovered under the floor of this sea and some of the world's most important shipping lanes also exist across it.

142. Caribbean Sea

The Caribbean Sea is a segment of the Atlantic Ocean. The average depth of this sea is about 8,685 ft. It is located in the tropics of the Western hemisphere. From the west, it is surrounded by Costa Rica and the Yucatán Peninsula of Mexico; from the south, coasts of Venezuela; from the north by the Greater Antilles islands of Cuba and Puerto Rico; and from the east by the Lesser Antilles chain. The Caribbean Sea is one of the world's largest seas and has the second biggest barrier reef in the world, called the Mesoamerican Barrier Reef. The entire area of the Caribbean Sea, the numerous islands of the West Indies, and adjacent coasts, are collectively known as 'the Caribbean'. The Caribbean is home to about 9% of the world's coral reefs.

143. Mediterranean Sea

The Mediterranean is an intercontinental sea, sometimes considered as a part of the Atlantic Ocean. It lies between three continents, Europe, Asia and Africa. The sea is bounded by the Mediterranean region almost completely by land. The Mediterranean Sea connects to the Atlantic Ocean via a narrow and shallow channel of the strait of Gibraltar. The Mediterranean is connected with various other seas, such as the Black Sea through the Dardanelles (with a sill depth of 70m), the Sea of Marmara, and the strait of the Bosporus (sill depth of about 90m), all at the northeast end. The famous Suez Canal connects it to the Red Sea at the southeast extremity.

144. Ocean

An ocean is a large expanse of sea that covers more than 75% of the entire Earth's surface. This vastness gives a blue appearance to our planet when viewed from space. The ocean bed is composed of sand, gravel, mud and sediments. The average salinity of an ocean is 3.49% of the weight of seawater. Although the ocean is one continuous body of water yet is divided into four main areas: the Pacific, Atlantic, Indian and Arctic Oceans. The Atlantic, Indian and Pacific Oceans merge into icy waters around Antarctica. They combine to form the fifth ocean, most commonly called the Southern Ocean (frozen ocean).

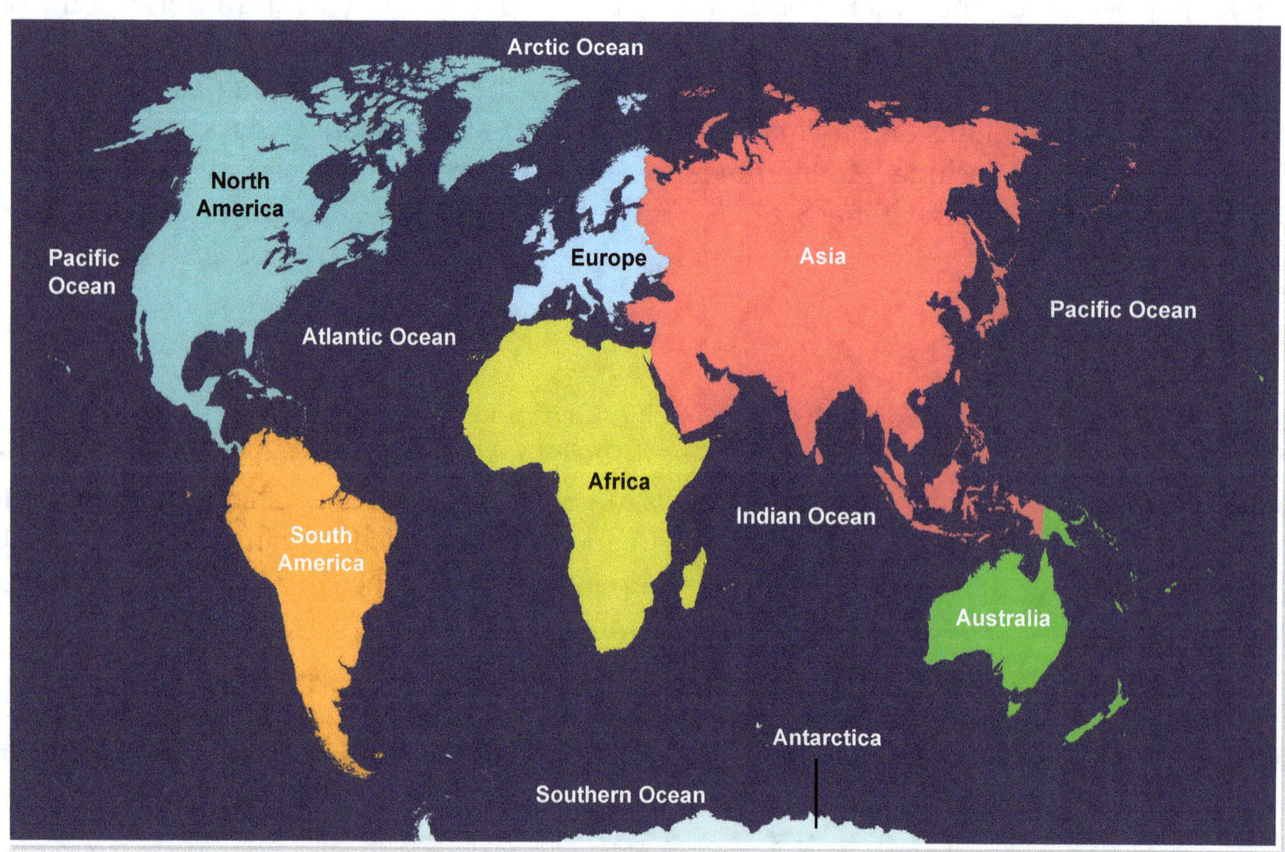

145. Pacific Ocean

The Pacific Ocean is the largest ocean. It covers 30% of the Earth's surface. The name 'Pacific Ocean' is derived from a Latin word *Tepre Pacificum*, which means 'peaceful sea'. It separates Asia and Australia from the Americas. The depth of the Pacific Ocean is about 14,050 feet. The basins of the Pacific have around 75% of the total volcanoes on the Earth. The major rivers that drain into the Pacific directly are: the Hwang Ho, the Yangtze, the Colorado and the Columbia. Thousands of islands are spread over the Pacific.

146. Atlantic Ocean

The Atlantic Ocean is the second largest ocean of the world. It covers about one-fifth or 20% of Earth's surface. To the east, it separates two continents Europe and Africa, and to the west North and South America. The name Atlantic comes from the Greek mythology, which means the *Sea of Atlas*. On the equator, it gets divided into two parts: the North Atlantic Ocean and the South Atlantic Ocean. The Missouri-Mississippi, the Amazon, the Congo and the Nile drain into this ocean.

147. Indian Ocean

The third largest ocean of the world's oceanic division is the Indian Ocean. It covers about one-fifth of the total ocean area of the world. It is the youngest and smallest ocean of the Earth and has the most complicated formation process. To the north Indian Ocean is bounded by Iran, Pakistan, and India and to the south to Antarctica. To the east and southeast its water mingles with those of the Pacific. The deepest point of this ocean is near Java, which is 24,442 feet. The Indian Ocean controls the climatic pattern of the entire South-East Asia zone.

Japan Current: A famous warm current passes the Japanese coast and flows northwards.

148. Ocean Currents

A permanent or continuous movement of ocean water which is circular in nature is called an ocean current. Ocean currents form close to the surface of the ocean and the speed of their rotation is 3.2 to 6.5 km per hour. These currents affect the temperature of the air near its surface and this, in turn, affects the nearby climate of land. The currents that are formed near the surface of the ocean help in the movement of heat from tropical regions to poles. At poles, the cold currents help move the cool water towards the equator. Warm currents that flow away from the equator are cooled by the cold Arctic currents.

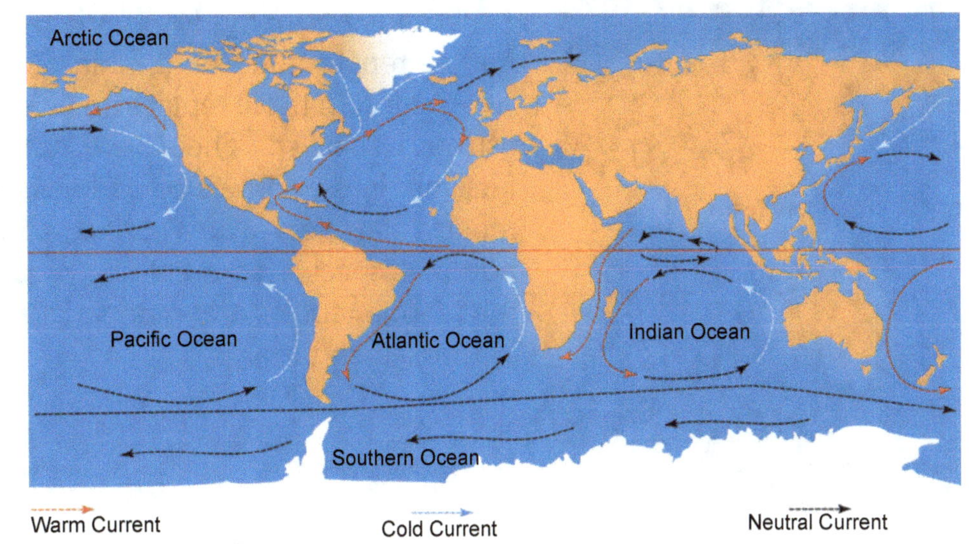

149. Sharks

Sharks are the huge group of ferocious fish found in both cold and warm waters. They live at a depth of 2,000 m or below in the oceans. A shark typically has a tough skin that is dull grey in colour and is roughened by tooth-like scales. It has a cartilaginous skeleton. In general, sharks do not live in fresh water, with the exception of the bull shark and the river shark. There are more than 400 living species of sharks. A few species, such as blue sharks, spend most of their time in the open ocean, whereas other species inhabit warmer, murky coastal waters. The Great White sharks are the largest and scariest sharks.

The baby of a shark is called a pup.

150. Whales and Dolphins

Whales and dolphins are well-known ocean animals. Whales are found in all the major oceans of the world, from the Arctic and Antarctic oceans to the oceans and seas around the centre of the equator. Whales and dolphins frequently come on the ocean surface for air, because they breathe through lungs. They are categorised under mammals. The offspring of whales and dolphins feed on their mothers' milk. The biggest animal on the Earth is the Blue Whale. It is 28 metres in length. A social group of a dolphin is called a pod and they hunt together for food such as squid or schools of smaller fish.

A baby whale is called a calf. The blue whale's calf feeds on mother's milk for about eight months.

Whale

Dolphins

151. Marine Reptiles

Oceans are home to a variety of reptiles, which are invertebrates. Marine reptiles are found mainly in oceans in tropical and subtropical zones. Most of these reptiles are ferocious hunters and hunt upon squid, fish and shellfish. They have scaly skins, sharp teeth, big eyes for farsightedness, flippers or paddles to swim, four limbs and tails. These reptiles stay near water surface so that they may breathe as they do not have specialised breathing organs to breathe underwater. Some of the marine reptiles are: marine iguanas, sea turtles, sea snakes, marine crocodiles and lizards.

Sea Turtles

Marine Iguana

152. Deep Ocean Topography

The ocean floor has many interesting physical features. The crust of the ocean floor is made up of a thin layer called basalt, a type of volcanic rock. The main features of the ocean floor are:

♦ Continental Shelf
♦ Continental Slope
♦ Ocean Bed and Continental Rise
♦ Trench

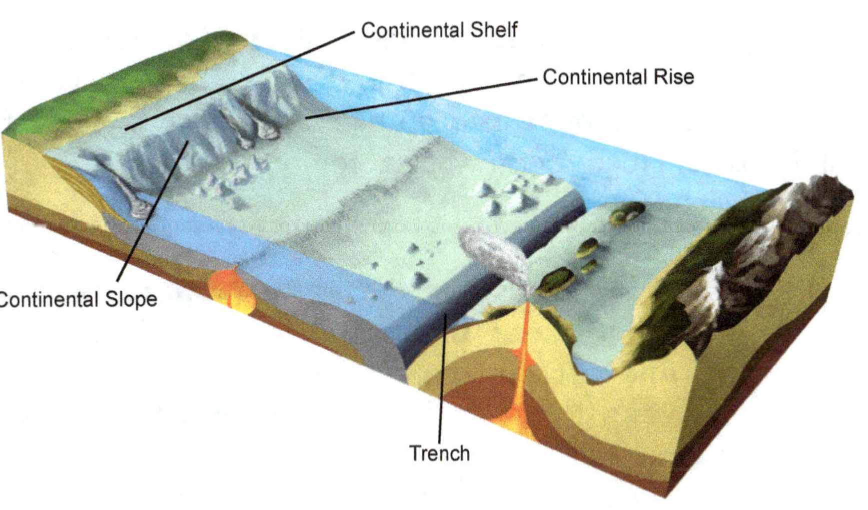

Ocean Trench is the area where the ocean floor has deep, narrow depressions. It is the deepest part of the ocean. One such deepest point is the Challenger Deep, which lies in the Mariana Trench in the Pacific Ocean. Its approximate depth is about 10,911m below the ocean's surface.

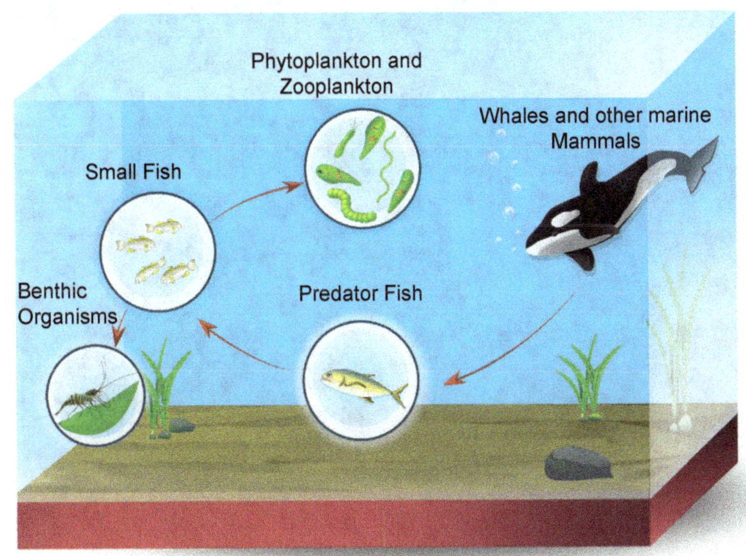

153. Ocean Life Zones

An ocean is full of life, starting from the surface of the ocean to the deepest ocean bed. Several species of animals and plants are found here, ranging from the microscopic algae (living things which cannot be seen by naked eyes) to the largest creature, the blue whale. The ocean has five major life zones categorised on the basis of the level of light they receive from the sun. These life zones support life of organisms that are uniquely adapted to the specific marine ecosystem.

154. The Epipelagic or Light Zone

The top layer, which is nearest to the Earth's surface, is called the epipelagic zone or the light zone. A lot of light penetrates in this zone. It is present up to a depth of 200m from the ocean surface. Due to sufficient sunlight, this zone supports photosynthesis. Most of the marine life exists in this zone, such as plankton, coral, bluefin tuna, jellyfish, etc.

A tuna fish has shiny scales on its body. These scales reflect the sunlight when the tuna swims swiftly and this movement, in turn, confuses the predator.

155. The Mesopelagic or Twilight Zone

The Mesopelagic zone, also called the twilight zone, is present at a depth of 200 to 1,000m in the ocean. There is no plant growth in this zone because very small amount of sunlight reaches here. As a result, this zone appears deep blue to black in colour. Animals that have adapted to the little light survive here. Huge sperm whales, comb jellies, sea pens, nautilus and a few large fish are inhabitants of the twilight zone.

Twilight zone fish are mostly small and luminous. The lantern fish is one such example. It has organs along its side that produce light.

156. The Bathypelagic or Dark Zone

The Bathypelagic zone is also called the dark or midnight zone as it receives no sunlight. It is present at a depth of 4,000m in the ocean. The animals living in this zone have huge mouths, sharp teeth and expandable stomachs, such as angler fish, tripod fish, fangtooth, snipe eel, opposom shrimp, black swallower and vampire squid. Plants and animals that die in the light and the twilight zone decompose and the debris falls downwards (marine snow) in the dark zone. It is a source of food for fish in the bathypelagic zone and the zones present below it.

157. The Abyssopelagic Zone

The bottom zone of the water is known as the abyssopelagic zone. This zone is mostly plain with sea mounts, trenches and valleys. This zone is very salty and cold (temperature = 2°C). It is present at a depth of 4000 to 6000m in the ocean. The pressure of water is very high in this zone (about 1,000 psi). Due to these extreme conditions, life for most animals is impossible. The fish in this zone have specialised jaws which allow them to drag their open mouths along the seafloor to find food, such as mussels, shrimp and microscopic organisms. Certain fish in this zone have bioluminescence.

158. The Hadalpelagic Zone

The Hadalpelagic zone is the deepest ocean zone, mostly in the form of trenches and canyons. The trenched hadal zone is mostly found in the Pacific Ocean. It is a total dark zone and found at a depth of about 6,000 to 11,000m. Tiny isopods, snailfish, sponges and sea cucumbers live in this zone They survive completely on the marine snow. These animals are adapted to the high water pressure.

Bioluminescent Organisms: These are the organisms which produce light through chemical reactions in their bodies.

159. Reef

Reef is a ridge (a long, narrow elevation of land) found near the surface of the ocean. Reefs are of two types, natural and artificial. Natural reefs are made up of plants, skeletons of small animals called corals, and other creatures of the water. Artificial reefs are man-made underwater structures built for the purpose of promoting marine life in areas of featureless bottom. There are several natural reefs, such as:

Live-bottom reef: It is a narrow horizontal surface of rock. Organisms such as sea anemones and seaweeds attach themselves directly to this rock, forming a live-bottom reef for fish and plants.

Oyster beds or shellfish reefs: These reefs consist of sea organisms named oysters (shelled sea animals). Oysters provide a hard surface, on which other organisms can grow. They provide protection for fish like gobies. These beds serve as a food source for animals like turtles. Oyster beds can be seen at low tide in the Chesapeake Bay in the United States.

Coral reef: One of the widespread reefs that contains 1/4th of the sea creatures and is home to billions of creatures.

Live-bottom Reef

Oyster Beds

160. Coral Reef

Coral reefs are underwater multicoloured limestone ridges made up of tiny sea animals called corals. Their hard outer skeletons (exoskeletons) are what make coral reefs. Coral reef ecosystems are diverse and comprise numerous species of sea creatures. They grow slowly at the rate of only a few centimetres each year. Some coral reefs that have been formed over millions of years are hundreds of metres thick.

161. Coral Animals

Coral animals are called polyps. Coral is the skeleton of these polyps which have hard and protective limestone skeletons at their base which is called calicle Polyps have many small tentacle like arms. Corals develop near the surface of the water as they require sunlight. They mostly feed on algal by-products but during night, these corals spread out their venomous tentacles and feed upon zooplankton and small fish. Coral reefs cover $\leq 1\%$ area of the whole ocean but they support more than 25% of the marine life.

Maldives is the coral island present in the Indian Ocean.

Zooplankton: They are small floating organisms that are slowly carried by water currents in oceans, seas, fresh water-bodies.

162. Type of Coral Reefs

Coral reefs can classified on the basis of their growth pattern.

- Fringing reefs are attached to the land and form a coral platform which extends into the ocean.

- Barrier reef is not attached to the land but it rises from the ocean and is separated from the land by a section of water called lagoon.

- Atoll is the most unique type of coral reef. It is a circular reef with lagoon at the centre.

Patch reefs are formed in shallow water and are visible at the time of low tide.

Fringing Reefs

Atoll Reef

163. Coral Zones

The coral growth in the ocean is divided into different zones:

Reef Flat Zone: It is the part where coral grows near the surface of the ocean. It's a habitat for animals like sea urchins and sea turtles.

Reef Crest: It lies between reef flat and fore reef zone. It is found away from the seas shore. The polyps living on the reef crest are adapted to strong waves and winds.

Fore Reef Zone: It is located at the oceanic side of the reef and is farthest from the sea shore. It has steep downward slopes. The coral growth here is affected by the availability of light.

164. The Great Barrier Reef

The Great Barrier Reef is the world's largest living structure built by animals. It is located on the north-east coast of Australia. It contains about 600 types of soft and hard corals, more than 1000 species of jellyfish, more than 4000 types of mollusc (snails, slugs and octopuses), and more than 30 species of whales and dolphins. This natural feature extends for more than 2300 km, and can be seen from the outer space. This reef has around 3000 small reefs and around 1000 islands associated. A unique animal named Dugong, an air breathing creature, swims in this reef and feeds on sea grass.

165. Mesoamerican Barrier Reef

The Mesoamerican Barrier Reef is the second largest reef of the world. It is also known as Belize Barrier Reef. This reef protects the coastal inhabitants from violent storms occurring in the ocean. The protective barrier of the reef is supported by a large area of mangrove that lines the coral coast. It is home to a large diversity of plants and animals, and is one of the most diverse ecosystems of the world. It is comprised of 70 hard coral species, 36 soft coral species, 500 species of fish, and hundreds of invertebrate species. Some of the interesting species are: bottlenose dolphins, pretty queen angelfish, and even whale sharks.

166. Seashore

Seashore is also called an oceanic coast or a sea coastline or marine coastline. It is a broad area of land along the edge of a sea or an ocean. This is the area where land meets a sea or an ocean. The total length of the seashore all over the world is more than 700,000 km. However, some seashores are not present along the edges of the islands or the continents. They are present at the inland water-bodies such as in the Caspian sea and the Dead sea. The different kinds of seashores are: cliff seashore (surrounded by tall upright rocks), beaches (gentle sloped edges covered with sand) and coral shores (lined by corals).

167. Features of Seashore

The interaction of land and sea creates various topographical features of geographical importance. Some of these features are rocks-formed by erosion due to waves and some are shore-related features formed by sedimentation or shore-eroding forces of the waves.

♦ The most common features of seashore are beaches. They are made up by sedimentation of eroded material that has been transported from elsewhere and deposited by the sea.

♦ The second are spits that are created by the deposition. They are actually extended stretches of beach material that project out in the sea and all joined to the coastal plain at one end.

♦ A spit that connects an island to the mainland is known as a tombolo.

Chesil Beach, which connects the Isle of Portland to the mainland of the Dorset coast, is an example of tombolo.

168. Beach

A narrow and gently sloping strip of land moving along the edge of an ocean, or sea is known as a beach. A beach contains sand, pebbles, rocks and seashell fragments. Weathering, erosion, sedimentation, wave currents, tides and ocean currents are the main creators of a beach.

Sandy beaches are a result of sedimentation, when eroded bits of rock and mud gather together. The life of sandy beach is beneath the surface. Common habitants of sandy beaches are: shrimps, lugworms, scallops and heart urchins. Tides also play an important role in building beaches. High tide brings a lot of debris along with it and when the high tide water recedes, it leaves behind a ribbon of debris, called strandline.

169. Waves

A wave is the movement of the ocean's surface water. Wind is the main causative agent of waves. The energy of the wind moves the waves towards the seashore. As the wave approaches the seashore, the speed is slowed down due to the sand and rocks present on the beach. The size of the wave indicates the origin of its formation. Steep waves are young waves made by local winds, whereas steady-looking slow waves originate from far-away places. Huge waves formed during a storm can be disastrous.

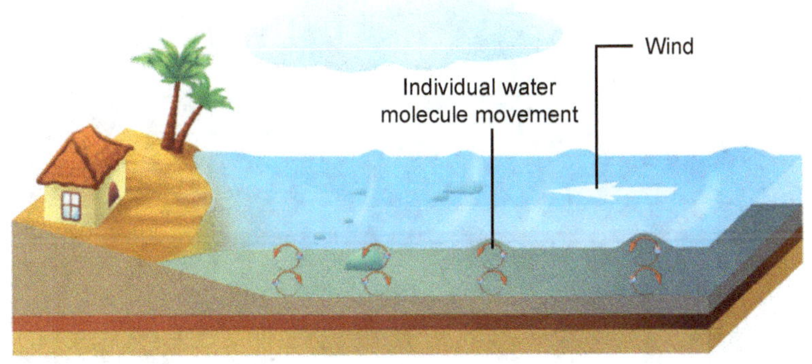

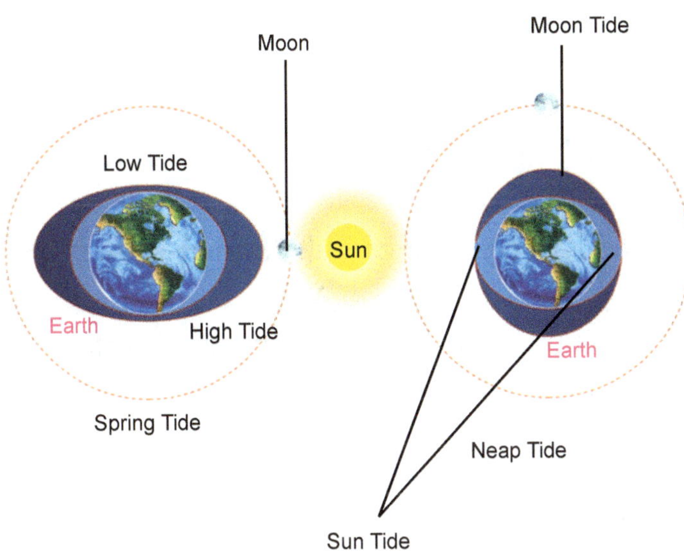

170. Tides

Tides are rhythmic rise and fall of the ocean's water. They take place twice a day. There are two types of tides: high (when the water rises to its highest level and covers much of the seashore) and low (when the water falls to its lowest level and moves away from the shore) tide. Tides occur due to the gravitational pull of the Moon and the Sun. Moon pulls the nearest water-body towards it and a broad swell or a wave is created. During new Moon and full Moon, the Sun and the Moon are in the same line with the Earth and the pull of the wave is the highest, which is known as Spring Tide. And when the Moon is in its first and last quarter, the ocean water is drawn in diagonally opposite directions by the gravitational pull of the Sun and low tides are experienced. These are called Neap Tides.

171. Lagoons

A lagoon is a shallow body of water separated from a larger body of water by sandbars, barrier islands or coral reefs.

Lagoons can be divided into two categories:

Coastal Lagoons: These are formed along flat or gently sloping landscape coastlines protected by sandbars or barrier islands.

Atoll Lagoons: They are similar to coastal lagoons but are protected by coral reefs.

Flamingos are the tallest inhabitants of coastal lagoons.

172. Mangrove Swamps

Mangroves are medium height trees and shrubs that grow in saline coastal habitats in tropical and subtropical regions. These regions are swampy and are permanently filled with water. There are about 68 species of mangrove trees in the world. The Indo-West Pacific region is the mangrove dominant area with the greatest diversity of species–30 to 40 species. The mangrove trees have specialised roots to get oxygen from the air. These trees are a habitat for roosting birds, land crabs, fishing cats and proboscis monkeys.

173. Estuary

Estuary is the point where a river ends and meets the sea. Estuaries have brackish water which is not so salty as the ocean water.

There are four kinds of estuaries:

- Coastal plain estuaries are created during heavy rain, when the sea level rises and fills a nearby river valley. Example: Hudson River in New York

- Tectonic estuaries are created by the movement of tectonic plates. Example: San Francisco Bay, on the West Coast of the United States.

- Bar-built estuaries are built when a barrier island is built by the ocean waves near a coastal area which has river streams flowing in it. Example: Nauset Barrier Beach System in Cape Cod, Massachusetts.

- Fjord estuaries are created by glaciers. Fjords are also found throughout Canada, Chile, Greenland, New Zealand. Examples: Glacier Bay in Alaska and the Georgia Basin region of Puget Sound in Washington State.

174. Deltas

Deltas are formed at the river end when the river slows down and sediments start settling down. These sediments accumulate and form a spread-out area. Some rivers deposit so much sediment that waves and tides cannot carry it all away, and a huge delta is built. The term delta is derived from a Greek letter *delta* (Δ), which is shaped like a triangle. When these deltas resemble an arc, they are called arc-deltas (arcuate). The Nile River forms an arcuate delta while emptying into the Mediterranean Sea. The Nile delta is a very important farming area in Egypt.

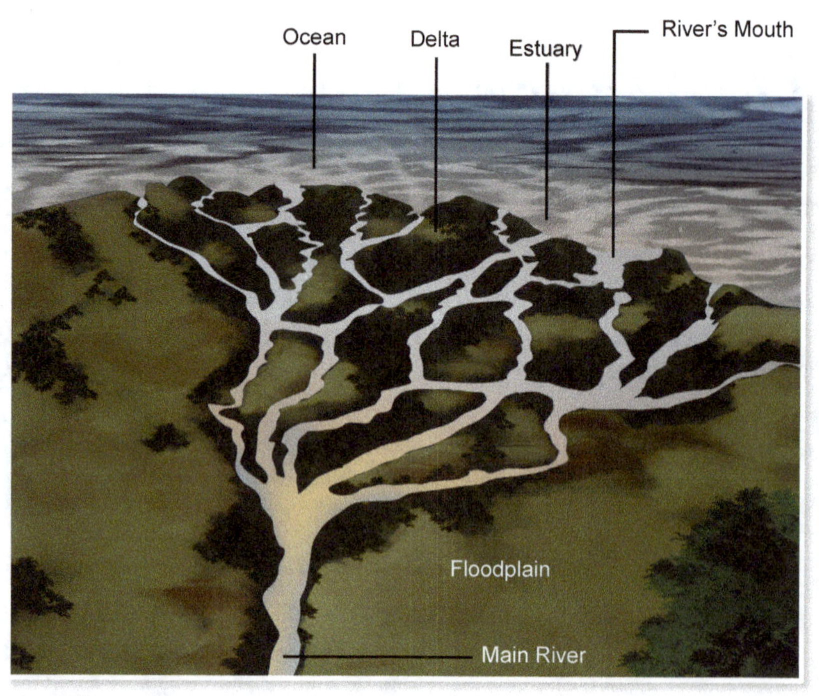

175. Rocks

A rock is a natural substance made up of solid crystals of different minerals. Rocks are formed when different minerals join together and make a solid lump. Every rock has a unique structure. There are certain rocks that are made up of only one mineral. For example, limestone rock contains only calcite mineral, while granite is made up of quartz and feldspar. The common minerals present in a rock are: silicates, carbonates and sulphides. There are three basic types of rocks: igneous, sedimentary and metamorphic.

176. Igneous Rocks

Igneous rocks are made up by the solidification of the Earth's volcanic material, molten magma. The word igneous is derived from the Latin word *Ignis* which means 'fire born'. These rocks are formed when the magma cools down either under the Earth's surface or lithosphere (intrusive rocks) or above the Earth's surface (extrusive igneous rocks). Inside the Earth, these rocks are formed when the magma is squeezed between the layers of the Earth followed by slow cool-down and solidification. These types of rocks have grainy structure with large crystals. Above the surface, these rocks are formed when the molten magma flows on the surface through a vent and spreads and cools rapidly. These types of rocks have smooth texture with fine crystals. The four types of igneous rocks are: granite, obsidian, basalt and pumice.

Granite

Pumice

Obsidian

Basalt

The four types of igneous rocks are: granite, obsidian, basalt and pumice. Almost 95% of the Earth's crust is made up of igneous rocks.

Gypsum

Sandstone

Limestone

177. Sedimentary Rocks

Sedimentary rocks are formed by the sediments of rocks and remains of plants and animals. Flowing rivers carry pieces of broken rocks and deposit them in lakes or seas. Slowly these deposits settle in sea bed. Rock fragments and remains of plants and animals are squeezed together due to water pressure, and eventually they get glued together. It is a very slow process and takes millions of years to get formed. The oldest layers of these rocks are at the bottom. The three main types of sedimentary rocks are: sandstone, gypsum and limestone. Other examples are: chalk and shale.

178. Metamorphic Rocks

Metamorphic (*meta* means 'form' and *morphic* means 'change') rocks are the transformed form of igneous or sedimentary rocks. They are formed when these rocks experience intense heat and pressure deep inside the Earth's crust. For example: limestone (sedimentary) converts to marble (metamorphic) when it comes in contact with high heat and pressure.

Metamorphic rocks are commonly found in mountainous regions because in these regions these rocks have come out on the surface during mountain formation.

179. Rock Cycle

Rocks are formed through various natural processes such as weathering, erosion or movement of tectonic plates. One type of rock gradually interchanges and recycles to form another type of rock. This change is called rock cycle. It is a very slow process.

♦ Solidification of molten magma produces igneous rocks.

♦ These igneous rocks break down due to natural forces and the sediments are transported from one place to another through air or water.

♦ The deposited sediments get compressed and form sedimentary rocks.

♦ When these rocks (igneous or sedimentary) experience high heat or pressure, they get converted into metamorphic rocks.

♦ And again, these metamorphic rocks under high heat and pressure melt to form molten magma.

♦ This way, the rock cycle continues.

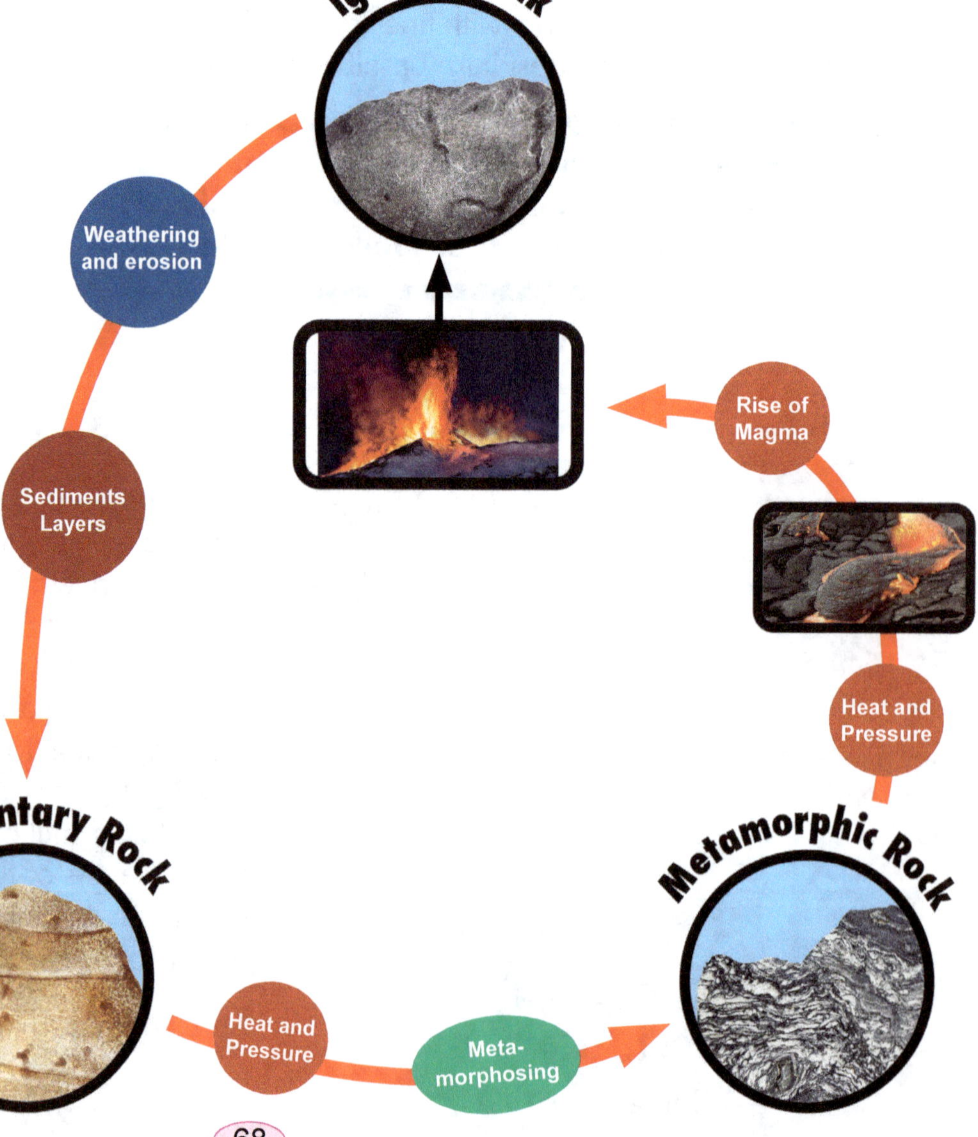

180. Minerals

Minerals are naturally occurring substances formed by geological processes. They are found in the uppermost layer of the Earth's crust. Some minerals are formed from molten magma, such as diamond, mica and feldspar. Some are found in places such as in rocks, in sand or in gravels. There exist more than 2800 different varieties of minerals on the Earth. Minerals are generally identified on the basis of colour, transparency, lustre, streak, crystal form, cleavage and hardness. Most of the minerals have a crystalline structure.

Minerals are divided into two major groups: metallic and non-metallic. Metallic minerals include: iron, cobalt, bauxite, etc. Non-metallic minerals include: mica, feldspar, salt, etc. The third category of mineral is energy mineral that constitutes coal, petroleum and natural gas, although they are categorised as fossil fuels.

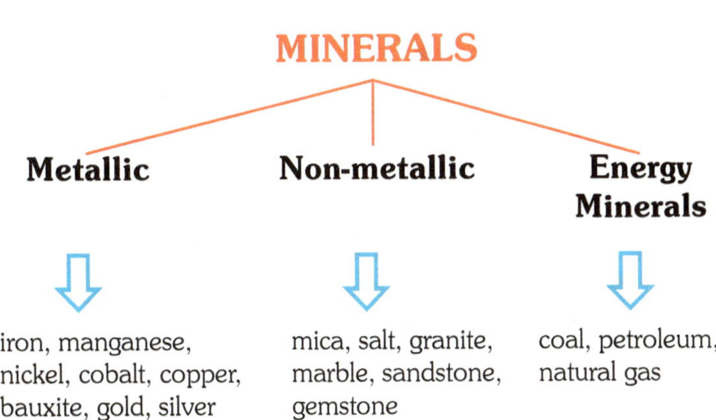

181. Metallic Minerals

Metallic minerals contain metallic elements which can be melted to form new products. These minerals are obtained from mines in raw form, called ores (metal + impurities). To extract metals from these ores, they are physically and chemically processed.

There are about 2800 known minerals on the Earth. Each one is a unique substance with its own chemical formula.

Metal	Region of abundance
Iron ore (Ferrous)	Brazil, Russia, Europe
Tin (Non-ferrous)	China, India
Bauxite (Non-ferrous)	Australia
Copper	Western Cordilleras, US
Gold	South Africa

182. Ferrous and Non-ferrous Minerals

Ferrous minerals are iron-rich minerals. They are less stable and more prone to rapid decomposition than non-ferrous minerals because they are formed under high pressure and temperature. Ferrous minerals usually tend to become dark and heavy. Iron ore, manganese and chromites are the examples of ferrous minerals. India is fairly rich in the deposits of ferrous minerals. On the other hand, minerals that do not contain iron are known as non-ferrous minerals. Important non-ferrous minerals include aluminium, copper, lead, nickel, tin, titanium and zinc, and alloys such as brass.

Gold Nuggets

183. Precious Minerals

Gold, silver and platinum are precious metals. These metals have low density, higher conductivity, are non-magnetic in nature. They hold a high economic value.

Gold is a soft and yellow-coloured metal. It is found in its natural form called 'nuggets'. Silver, a white-coloured soft metal, occurs in combination with sulphur, copper, lead or arsenic. Platinum is a dense, expensive, and relatively rare, silvery-white metal.

Africa is the largest producer of gold and platinum. And, South America has large deposits of silver.

184. Gems

Gems are the most valuable, durable, beautiful, and rare crystals. There are about 80 known gems. They are divided into two categories: precious and semi-precious. Precious gems include: diamond, ruby, emerald and sapphire. Semi-precious gems include: opal, amethyst and topaz.

Most of the gems are made up of combination of a substance called silicate. Diamond is the most precious and simplest gem among all. It is made up of pure carbon. Ruby and sapphire are composed of aluminium oxide (corundum).

Emerald is one of the earliest and highly prized gems. Gems are described on the basis of 4 C's: clarity, colour, cut and carat (weight).

Amethyst

Emerald

Ruby

Sapphire

185. Diamond

Diamond is the hardest and purest natural substance known to man till date. Diamonds are made up of carbon. They were formed millions of years ago under the surface of the Earth (more than about 120 km below). Carbon present in the rocks inside the Earth underwent crushing pressure and intense heat. This extreme condition crystallized carbon. And diamond was formed.

Diamond has a unique crystalline structure that reflects light in a unique manner. It is a hard metal but it can be cut and modified in various shapes and designs.

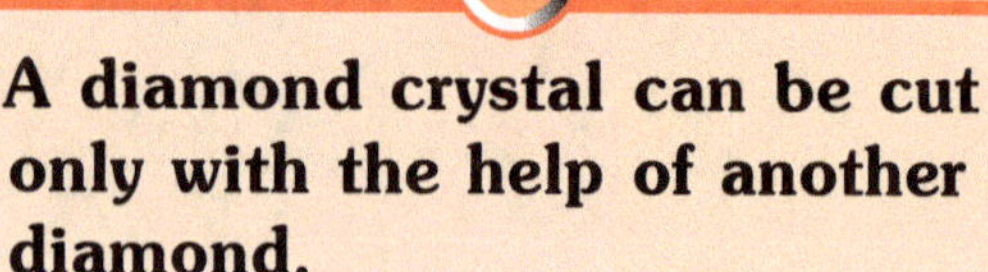

A diamond crystal can be cut only with the help of another diamond.

186. Fossils

Fossils are the evidence of ancient life. The word fossil is derived from a Latin word *fossus*, which means 'having been dug up'. Fossils are the remains or traces of remains of the actual bodies of the organisms, such as bones, shells, feathers and leaves, which have been preserved from decay, and which appear just as they were originally. Most fossils are in form of rock impressions or in form of traces. A very few are available as whole structure.

187. Formation of Fossils

Fossil formation starts after the death of an animal. About 100 million years ago, some invertebrates died and sank in the sea-bed. Some of the remains of these animals got deeply buried in mud or sand. Due to immense pressure, sandstone formation took place. These stones had traces of these animals. The same procedure took place with all the past animals. After hundreds of millions of years, when some of the rocks were cut away in small pieces by erosion or water flow, some of the fossils got exposed. Scientists say that we may get to explore more and more old fossils if we dig deeper.

188. Types of Fossils

The two main categories of fossils are: body fossils and trace fossils.

Body fossils are the remains of bones, teeth, shells of an animal, or leaves of a plant. They are further divided into two categories: mould and cast fossil.

Trace fossils are just the impressions of an animal or plant created when it was buried. For example, the imprint of an ancient leaf or footprint is a trace fossil.

Mould Fossil

Trace Fossil

189. Fossil Animals: Invertebrates

Invertebrates, the animals without backbones, first appeared on the Earth during the Cambrian period. The most common early animals were arthropods, the trilobites. They were soft-bodies animals living mostly in the sea. Another important fossils of invertebrates found during the Paleozoic time were molluscs, echinoderms, crinoids (sea lilies: cup-shaped body), starfish and corals. Fossils of these animals were found all over the world including some parts of Antarctica.

190. Fossil Animals: Vertebrates

Vertebrates, the animals with backbones, first appeared on the Earth during the Palaeozoic period. Agnathids were the oldest vertebrates which resembled fish. Rocks from late Palaeozoic period revealed 75 different species of amphibians. Most of the fossils resembled today's salamanders. Body, cast and trace fossils of dinosaurs have been found during exploration. Fossils of the huge woolly mammoths that existed in Cenozoic era are also found. One such entirely preserved fossil of a mammoth was found in Alaska.

191. Fossil Plants

Fossil plants are older than fossil animals. They are mostly found as trace fossils in sedimentary rocks of land or freshwater origin. The first plants were related to the blue green algae family and they are probably 2 billion years old. A plant and its parts cannot become a fossil until they are quickly buried into some sediment layer or ice sheet. This quick burial process of plant prevents it from decay. Some of the fossil plants are herb like rushes, Rhynia, ferns, seed ferns and fern-like plants.

192. Ice Age

About 2.6 million years ago, a unit of time named the quaternary period (the current and most recent of the three periods of the Cenozoic era) began. This period has been characterised by a long-term reduction in the temperature of the Earth's surface or time of glaciation or ice age. During that period, the Earth got covered with large thick ice sheets. The probable reasons behind it could be changes in ocean currents, atmosphere or in position of the Earth around the Sun.

193. Dinosaurs

Dinosaurs mean 'terrible lizards'. They were one of the most successful species ever to survive on the Earth. They were the well-known reptiles of the Mesozoic era. They ranged from being herbivores, carnivores to omnivores. They were different from early reptiles due to the following features: (1) Dinosaurs had their legs under their bodies. (2)They walked and ran fast and became the dictators of that era. The first bird, the Archaeopteryx, had features resembling a flying dinosaur appeared in Jurassic period.

194. Types of Dinosaurs

The various dinosaur families are as follows:

Saltoposuchus (Mesozoic era) were the first reptiles to walk on hind legs and hold things with short front legs.

Ichtyosaurs, Plesiosaurs were fish-like lizards which swam in seas with paddle-shaped front legs. They breathed through lungs.

Diplodocus (Jurassic period) were the largest plant-eating dinosaurs that were about 90 feet tall.

Tyrannosaurus (Cretaceous period) were the most fearsome animals that stood up to a height of 20 feet. Their teeth were 6 inches long.

Triceratops has large head covered with bony shields.

195. Dinosaurs: Around the World

Dinosaurs lived all over the globe since the continents were joined together and there existed one huge landmass (Pangaea). Remains of the dinosaurs were found in different places all over the world. For example, Tyrannosaurus Rex (ferocious dinosaur) was found in North America and Asia. Staurikosaurus (one of the oldest dinosaurs) was found in South America. Barosaurus was found in Africa and Asia. Iguanodon was found in Europe. Tuaziangosaurus (had spikes all along its spine) was found in China, Asia. And Minmi (body covered with hard plates, armoured dinosaur) was found in Australia.

196. Fossil Fuels

Fossil fuels were formed hundreds of millions of years ago from minerals found in the remains of plants and animals. The process of fossil fuel formation is very slow. They are non-renewable (things that cannot be replaced when used) resources of the Earth. They are categorised into three main types: coal, oil and natural gas. Coal is a solid fuel which is found in mines. Crude oil is drilled out from seas or from offshore sources. And natural gas is pumped out from offshore and onshore sources.

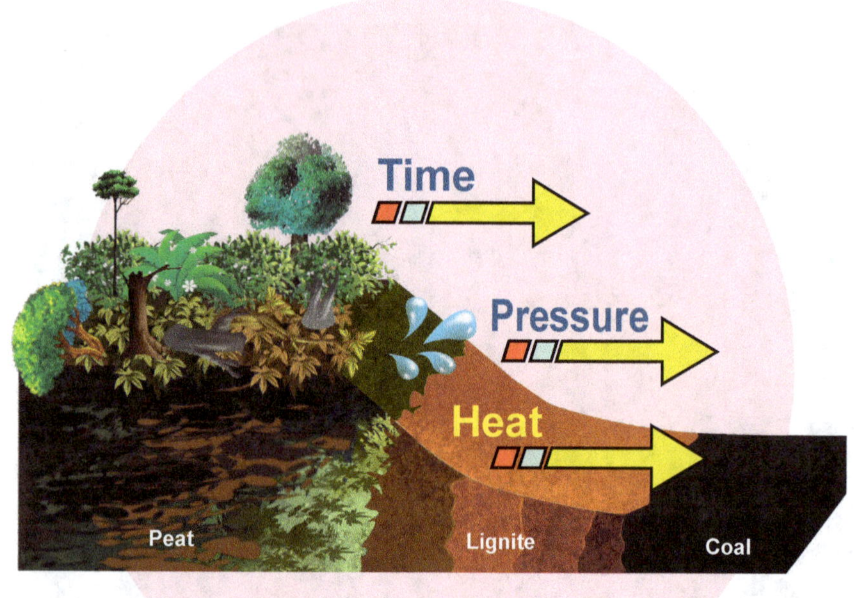

197. Coal

Coal is a black or brownish-black sedimentary rock formed from the remains of plants and other organisms, which were covered with mud and sand. Millions of years ago, the Earth's surface was covered with swampy forests. These forests got buried under the soil due to excessive flooding. Gradually, due to the high pressure, the overlying mud and sand squeezed out most of the liquid, leaving behind a pasty mass called peat. Slowly, peat hardened to form lignite and then coal. Three types of coal are: Lignite (low grade), bituminous (high grade) and anthracite (highest quality hard coal).

198. Petroleum

Petro means rock and *oleum* means oil. Thus petroleum means rock oil as it is obtained from the Earth (either ocean floor or continental crust). The natural unprocessed form of petroleum is called crude oil.

Petroleum was formed from the dead remains of aquatic animals. The bodies of these animals got buried in the ocean floor. They got covered with sand and clay. Slowly, minerals inside these remains under extreme conditions and absence of oxygen changed into petroleum. Crude oil is a mixture of various constituents such as petrol, diesel, lubricating oil, petroleum gas, paraffin wax, etc.

199. Natural Gas

Natural gas is a fossil fuel which is in gaseous form. The formation process of natural gas is similar to that of petrol and its stores are procured along with crude oil. Natural gas-rich sedimentary basins are found all over the world. Some of natural gas fields are: the deserts of Saudi Arabia, the humid tropics of Venezuela and the freezing Arctic. It is used for burning and incineration in industries, transport purposes, and as an alternative fuel for cars, buses, trucks and other vehicles. The compressed form of natural gas (CNG) is used for power generation.

200. Soil

The uppermost thin layer covering the Earth's surface is called soil. Soil is composed of rock particles, mineral fragments, remains of the dead, living things, water and air.

The soil has five layers: humus, topsoil, subsoil, rock fragments and bedrock. There are four basic types of soil: sand, loamy, silt and clayey.

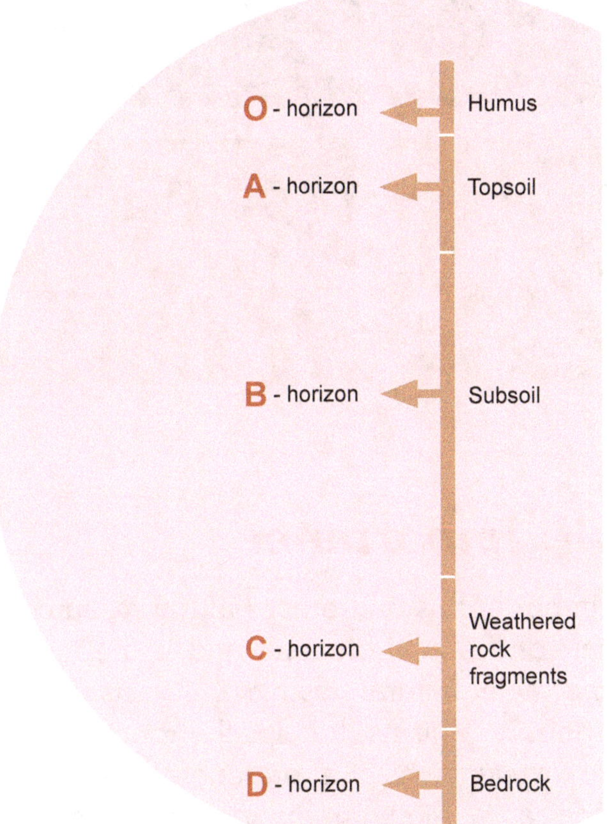

201. Soil Profile

Soil present on the surface of the Earth is actually present in layers. The various layers are:

O: It is the topmost fertile layer, rich in humus. It is soft, porous and retains a lot of water. It is a natural habitat of many worms and insects.

A: It has less humus and more minerals.

B: It is slightly hard and compact.

C: This layer has lumps of rocks. These rocks are cracked and have crevices.

D: Bedrock is the hardest layer that cannot be dug by spade.

202. Humus

Humus is dark, organic material, made up of decayed debris of dead animals and plants. It is a natural nutrient-source of plants. It takes several years for fertile soil to take shape. The main components of fertile soil are: leaf litter, twigs and other material, and remains of dead animals. These dead parts decay due to the action of bacteria. Eventually, the decomposed material turns black or brown in colour. Earthworms often help mix humus with minerals in the soil.

203. Formation of Soil

Soil formation is a long process. It is formed by continuous weathering of rocks. The main causative agents of rock weathering are: sun, rain, water, wind, moving ice, strong waves, plant growth and atmospheric gases. The cracking and crumbling of rock is the initial step of soil formation. Water and wind rub rocks against one another and carry them to narrow places. These rock particles further break into very small pieces. And slowly, fine particle soil is made.

204. Types of Soil

Soil is classified according to colour, size and texture of soil particles. There are mainly four types of soil:

- Sandy soil has more sand and no humus.
- Clayey soil is usually brown in colour. It has more clay than sand particles.
- Loamy soil is a mixture of clayey soil, sandy soil and humus. It is a plant friendly soil.
- Silt is a grainy but non-rocky soil. It is one of the most fertile soils.

205. Soil: Importance

Soil is as important as any other natural resource. It is a vital part of the environment, and is the most important renewable natural resource. It acts as a habitat for various organisms. It helps the roots of the plants to take oxygen which is present between its particles. It acts as a medium for various physical, chemical and biological processes to take place.

206. Soil Erosion

Soil erosion is a process of the removal of the topmost layer (the fertile layer) of the soil. Natural erosion agents are wind, rainfall, temperature, movement of ice, flow of water and related natural disasters. Bare soil is more prone to erosion.

Factors responsible for soil erosion are:

Deforestation: Excessive cutting of plants is known as deforestation. The roots of the plants bind the soil. Deforestation leads to increase in soil erosion, as the soil is left exposed to the agents of erosion.

Overgrazing by animals: Animals destroy the vegetation and soil is left bare which makes the soil highly susceptible to erosion.

207. Environment

Environment is everything that surrounds a living organism and affects it during its lifetime. It is a sum of physical, biological and chemical factors present on the Earth. Environment can be classified into three broad types: biotic, abiotic and cultural. Biotic factors include biological components of the ecosystem, such as plants, animals, micro-organisms, etc. Abiotic factors include physical factors such as water, land, air, climate, temperature, etc. And cultural factors mean the suitable surroundings made by humans for themselves.

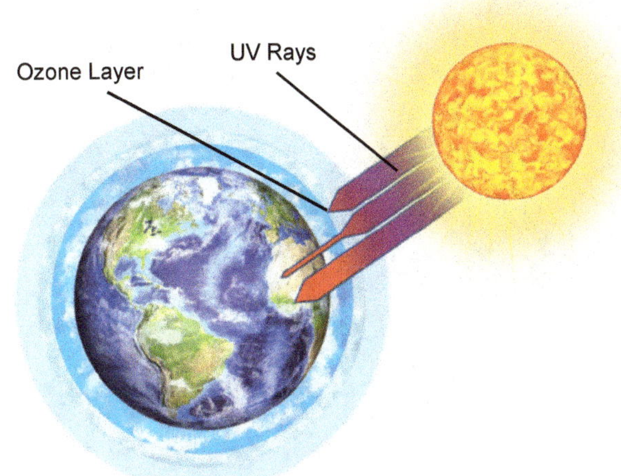

208. Ozone Layer

Ozone is a gas present in the upper part of the stratosphere. The ozone layer is a belt of ozone gas, which absorbs about 98% of the devastating ultraviolet (UV) radiation. It absorbs these rays like a sponge. There exists a balance between conversion of oxygen to ozone and ozone to oxygen in the stratosphere. However, this balance is disturbed by the chlorofluorocarbons (CFCs: used as refrigerant in refrigeration industry). CFCs disrupt the ozone formation.

209. Greenhouse Effect and Global Warming

Greenhouse effect is the naturally occurring heating of the Earth's surface. The sun's radiation enters the Earth's surface; 1/4th is reflected by clouds and rest falls on the Earth. The surface re-emits the heat in form of infrared radiations. Some infrared radiations are absorbed by atmospheric gases or greenhouse gases (CO_2, CH_4 etc.). These gases radiate the heat and eventually, the Earth gets heated up once again. This cycle goes on. Increase in the level of these gases increases the overall temperature. It is called global warming.

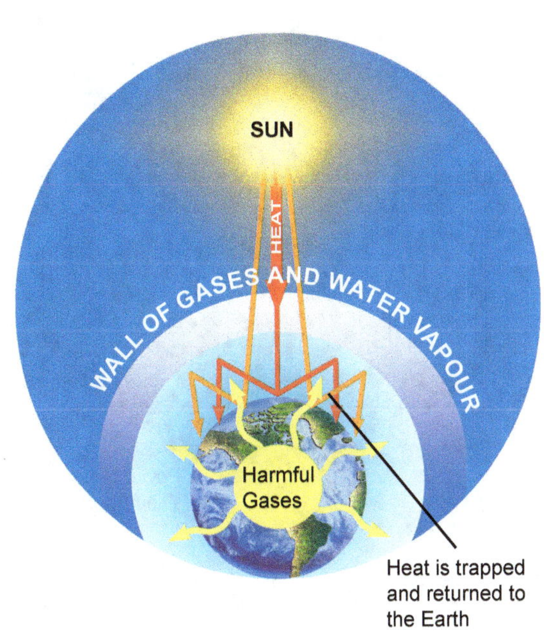

210. Pollution

Pollution means an undesirable change in the environment. The word pollution is derived from a Latin word *pollure*, meaning making unclean. There are two types of pollutants: natural pollutants (volcanic ash, forest fire) and man-made pollutants (trash or runoff produced by factories, automobiles, etc). Pollution is classified into: air, water and soil pollution.

211. Renewable Energy Sources

Renewable energy is the energy that can be replenished. Some of the renewable energy sources are solar energy, wind energy, geothermal (Earth's natural hot spots) energy and biomass energy. These resources can be utilised to generate electricity. The energy produced by these sources is also termed as non-conventional energy. These resources are also termed as environment-friendly resources because they do not produce any harmful by-products such as smoke, chemicals, etc.

212. Solar Power

The sun has been radiating an enormous amount of energy for billions of years. But only a very small part of it reaches the outer layer of the Earth's atmosphere. The heat energy of the sun that reaches the Earth's surface can be harnessed and converted into electricity. There are various equipment which help utilise solar energy, such as solar heaters (heating water), solar cookers (cooking food), solar dryers (drying grains and clothes) and solar lightings.

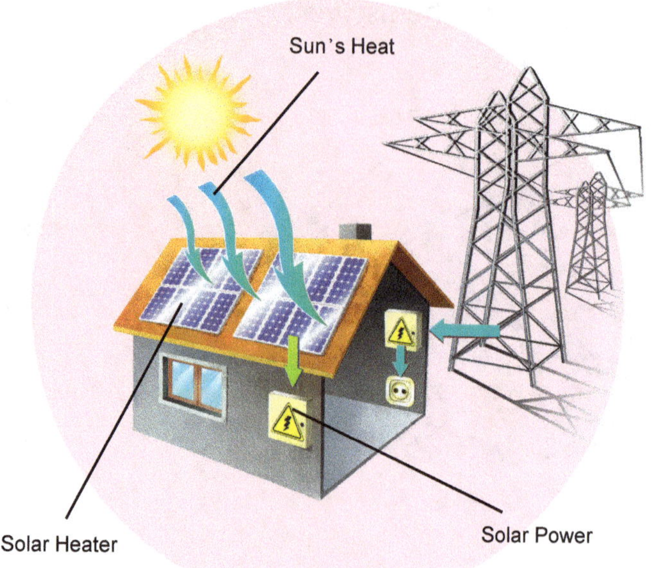

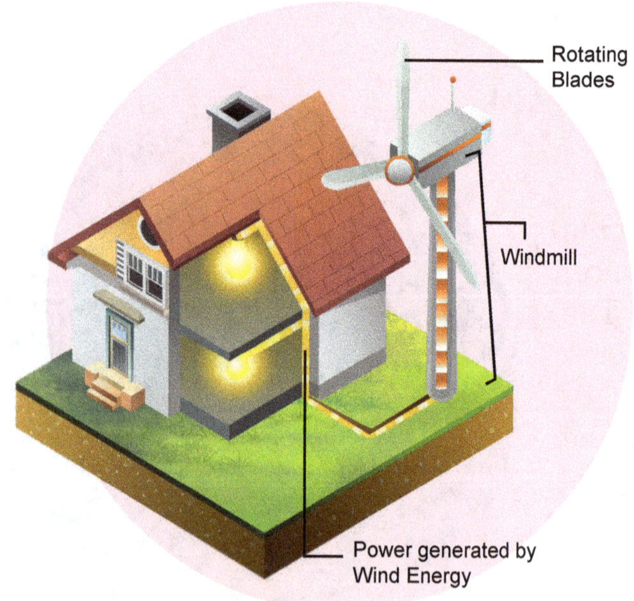

213. Wind Energy

Moving wind has an enormous amount of energy in it. Energy produced by moving air can be used and converted into electricity. Wind mills or wind turbines are used for converted wind energy into electrical energy. These turbines are long tubular towers that have rotating blades at the top. The blades are turned when wind blows and that energy is converted into electrical energy.

214. Biomass Energy

Biomass is biological or organic material. The common biomass materials are the remains of dead plants and animals, animal dung and kitchen waste. The biomass contains energy absorbed by the Sun which can be harnessed. The steps are: firstly, organic waste is collected in a biogas digester, where bacteria decompose the matter and produce biogas (CH_4 and CO_2). This gas is used as cooking fuel and the waste slurry acts as manure.

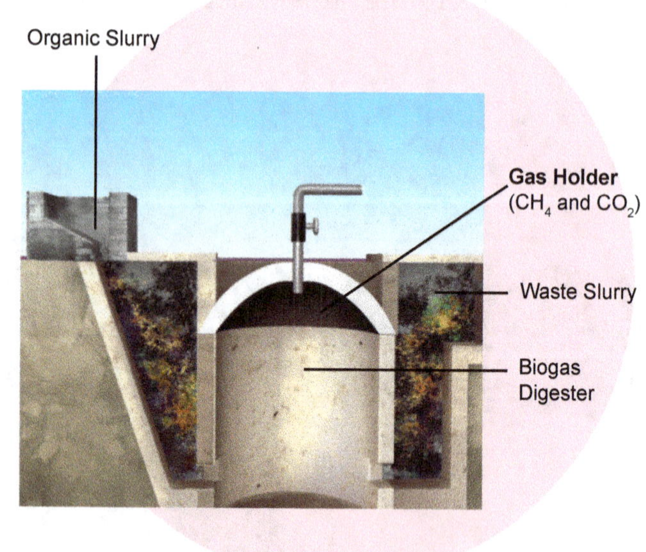

215. Hydropower

The word hydro means water and power means energy, hence hydropower is power generated by water. The main components of a hydropower plant are: water reservoir, turbine blades and generator. Water from height is made to fall through pipes on turbine blades. The blades then move and turn the generator. And the generator generates electricity. One-fourth of the world's electricity is produced by hydropower.

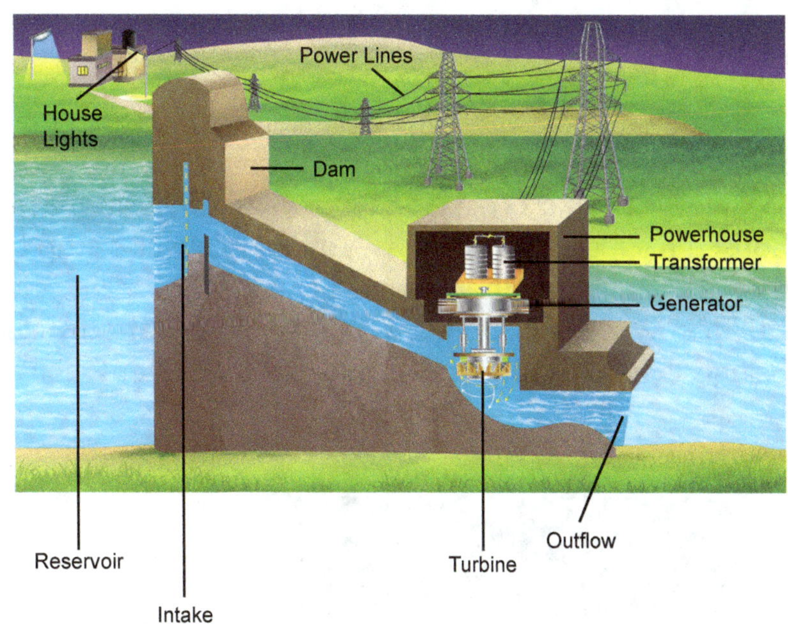

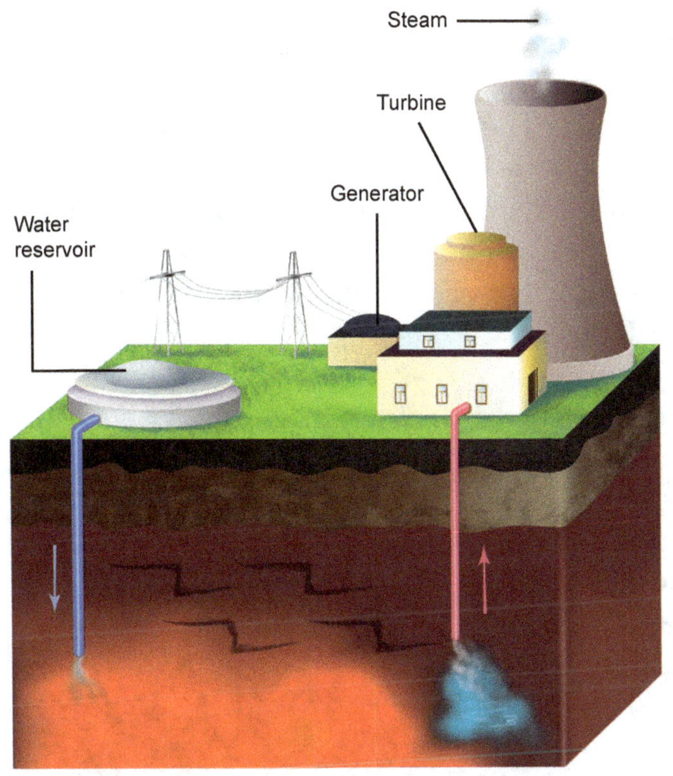

216. Geothermal Energy

The word 'Geo' means Earth and 'thermal' means heat. Deep inside the Earth, the temperature is very high. Due to this high temperature, the rocks are in molten state. When water present under the ground comes in contact with these hot molten rock spots, it gets converted into steam. And hot springs are formed. This energy can be used for generating electricity. There are a number of power plants based on geothermal energy in the United States and New Zealand, mainly.

217. Ocean Power

Ocean power is divided into three categories: tidal, wave and ocean thermal energy. Tidal energy is produced by the sudden powerful movement of ocean waters during the rise and fall of tides. Wave energy is generated by the kinetic energy possessed by the huge ocean waves. Ocean thermal energy is based on the difference in temperature of surface and deep ocean water. The water at the surface is heated by the sun while the water in deeper sections is relatively cold.

Underwater Turbines produce Electricity using Oceanic Power

218. Door to Hell

Door to hell is a 69-metre wide and 39-metre deep burning natural gas field, which has been burning for 5 decades. It is located in Darvaza, desert of north Turkmenistan. This area housed a substantial oil field. A drilling rig was set up to store the gas. However, the ground beneath the drilling rig soon collapsed and poisonous methane gas started releasing. Scientists tried to burn off the gas but the crater is still ablaze.

219. South China Karst

South China Karsts are unique landforms made up of limestone (chalk and calcium carbonate). These karsts are 270 million years old. They spread in about 550,000 km^2 area. These rocks are carved naturally as needles. They have caves, underground streams and sinkholes on the surface; steep rocky cliffs that stand tall and emerge vertically. Geologically, these Karsts evolved due to the tectonic uplift of Qinghai-Tibet Plateau.

220. Caves of Aggtelek and Slovak

Caves of Aggtelek and Slovak are located on the north-eastern border of Hungary and the south-eastern border of Slovakia. They are about 2 million years old and spread in an area of 600 km^2. These caves topographically comprise limestone plateaus dissected by deep river valleys. It is a rare combination of karst formation due to both tropical and glacial climatic effects. It has a most significant cave system named Baradla-Domica, which is a cross-border network richly decorated with stalagmites and stalactites.

221. Mount Etna

Mount Etna is the world's one of the most active and iconic stratovolcanos. It is located on the central-northern side of Sicily, Italy and is 2,700 years old. This volcanic mountain spreads in an area of 1,190 km^2. It looks like a gigantic cone in shape. It is a continuously erupting volcano with fairly frequent lava flow from craters and fissures on its sides. This mountain has a network of more than 250 caves.